out of war

THE EXCHANGE

Can living in
violent times
help you know
your true self?

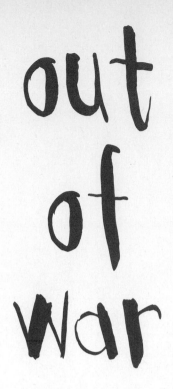

out of war

TRUE STORIES FROM THE FRONT LINES
OF THE CHILDREN'S MOVEMENT FOR PEACE IN COLOMBIA

SARA CAMERON
IN CONJUNCTION WITH UNICEF

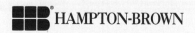

HAMPTON-BROWN

Hampton-Brown
P.O. Box 223220
Carmel, California 93922
800-333-3510
www.hampton-brown.com

Printed in the United States of America

ISBN-13: 978-0-7362-3139-8
ISBN-10: 0-7362-3139-0

06 07 08 09 10 11 12 13 14 15 10 9 8 7 6 5 4 3 2 1

To all
children
who live
with
violence

—S.C.

table of contents

introduction

For over forty years, Colombia has suffered through a violent war . Thousands of innocent people have died and millions have lost their homes. *Out of War*, by Sara Cameron, tells the story of brave Colombian children who joined together to form the Children's Movement for Peace. Through this movement , organized groups of youth worked together to try to bring peace to Colombia.

The war in Colombia is being fought by armed groups who want to take over the government. Many of the soldiers are guerilla fighters. These fighters are not recognized as a formal army. They typically do not wear a standard uniform. Guerilla fighters use surprise to wear down the government and the citizens. Their strength is their ability to strike anywhere. They conduct raids on towns or villages to get food. They rob trains for supplies. They are relentless.

The guerillas do not usually attack civilians. But that doesn't keep the citizens safe from harm. Ordinary people in a war-torn country often get caught in the middle of the violence

Key Concepts

war *n.* fighting between groups, usually lasting a long time

movement *n.* organized activities that support a common goal

when there is a **revolution**. They have very little power and a lot to fear. They are caught between the government and the guerillas who oppose the government. The citizens of Colombia have experienced this terrible situation.

Some of the stories in *Out of War* describe people who were

Colombia: Location of *Out of War*

Key Concepts

revolution *n.* attempt by many people to change a government ruler, system, or law

the victims of murders, rapes, and **kidnappings**. Other tactics of war cause less physical harm, but can be just as damaging. Blackmail is one example. People who are blackmailed are forced to pay "protection" money so that they and their families will not be harmed in the fighting. Other victims receive violent threats that force them to join a certain group. Perhaps the most effective weapon of war is fear. Many people support a leader or group because they have been threatened. They are afraid they will be harmed or killed if they oppose the leader or group.

Out of War was published in 2001. Sara Cameron wanted others to know the stories of the young activists who have tried to restore **peace** to Colombia. Through her efforts their stories were brought together in this book. Their stories show how the work of the peace movement impacted their lives. The last chapter, "Where Are We Now?," tells where the young activists were in 2001, when this book was first published.

In 2004, the military groups agreed to stop fighting. In March 2006, the largest of these groups finally turned over their weapons as part of the peace agreement. Since the agreement, peace has slowly been returning to Colombia. Yet some rebels continue to fight. Hundreds of citizens have been injured by grenades, land mines, and other weapons left in the mountains before the fighting stopped. Although this book only talks about what has happened up to 2001, the Children's Movement for Peace continued to help victims of war. Despite these efforts, Colombia still struggles for peace.

Key Concepts

kidnapping *n.* event in which a person is taken by force against his or her will

peace *n.* state of quiet; agreement to end a fight

from the author

Out of War tells the true stories of five young people who have experienced war and terrible violence, yet have chosen to work for peace. All of them are part of the Children's Movement for Peace in Colombia, which was nominated for a Nobel Peace Prize in 1998—and every year since.

The stories in *Out of War* describe the struggles of these young people as they try to **cope with some of the harshest** tests of life: Juan Elias with the **assassination** of his father; Farlis with **massacres** that are tearing her town apart.

Millions of children who live amidst war have similar experiences. The difference for these and thousands of other young Colombians is that they have refused to become a part of the violence themselves. Instead, they look for solutions that offer a way out of war, and in the process they have established an extraordinary movement.

The Colombian war has lasted more than forty years. It is a brutal conflict between many different armed groups who struggle for control over land and for power. All the armed groups have abused the rights of innocent people. About five thousand people are killed every year in the war and most of these are civilians. Massacres happen almost every week.

....

cope with some of the harshest deal with some of the most difficult

assassination killing

massacres multiple killings

Since 1985, more than two million people—one in twenty Colombians—have been forced to abandon their homes because of the war. And disappearances and kidnappings are widespread: In 1999 alone, more than three thousand people were kidnapped.

As deadly as the war is, even more people fall victim to the general violence of the society. Colombian cities have some of the worst murder rates in the world, due to the lack of justice and huge chasms between rich and poor, urban and rural populations.

The war expanded rapidly during the 1990s, **fueled largely by illegal drug money**—Colombia is the world's leading producer of cocaine. As **displaced families** poured into towns and cities, and kidnapping rates soared, the government and armed groups failed in their efforts to launch peace talks. Eventually, people tried to take peacemaking into their own hands.

By the mid-1990s, a peace network called Redepaz had brought hundreds of peace groups together in an effort to give greater power to the peace movement. And the Conciliation Commission, made up of important civic and religious leaders, had embarked on a series of peace talks with one of the guerrilla groups. This effort to launch peace talks was entirely separate from, and at the time much more successful than, any efforts by the government. Yet the peace movement as a whole was weak and divided into a patchwork of efforts—until the

....

fueled largely by illegal drug money paid for with money from selling drugs that are against the law

displaced families families that were forced to leave their homes

Children's Movement came along.

The Movement began with young people working in isolation, trying to make real contributions to peace, and it grew into a flood of millions **clamoring for** their rights to life and peace. It evolved without a formal structure—there is no official leadership and anyone under the age of eighteen, doing anything to improve the quality of life in a community affected by violence, is considered to be a member. The Movement's goal is very broad—to end the violence that is tearing Colombia apart, whether it is related to the war, to street violence, or to abuse inside the home. The Movement also strives to build unity among young people **across racial, economic, and geographic barriers**—unity that many adult Colombians lack.

The Children's Movement strengthened and focused the peace efforts of adults and helped to launch the country on a path towards fresh peace talks. Most importantly, though, it has begun to **lay the foundation** for peace in communities, schools, and families, which is essential if any political solution is ever to succeed.

This inspiring story of the Movement is best told through the individual stories of these courageous young people. As a policy of the Children's Movement, armed groups responsible for acts of violence are never identified by name. And, for their safety and protection, the full names and identities of the young people involved are not revealed.

....

clamoring for trying desperately to get

across racial, economic, and geographic barriers no matter what their race is, how rich they are, or where they live

lay the foundation complete the first steps

Juan Elias – 18

PEACE IS THE BEST REVENGE

My father was killed two weeks after my fifteenth birthday. Some men walked into his office and shot him and my cousin, Luche, who was helping out as a receptionist. She was nineteen years old.

They **laid the bodies in caskets** in the living room of our house in Aguachica, a small town in northeast Colombia. Many people came to **pay their respects** but one morning I was in there alone. I stood looking at my father and Luche, side by side in their coffins, and I remember thinking, "Why *two* in my family? In plenty of families one person gets murdered, so why two in my family? And why my dad? *Why my dad!* And why Luche?"

Luche had never done anything to anyone. Neither had my dad. He was a good man. He **gave his services** as a dentist free to families who could not afford to pay. And Luche had hardly begun to live. She had wanted to become a doctor. That was why she was helping him at the office.

I was supposed to have been with them as well. That morning, as my father rushed to work, I ran after him, calling, "Let me come. There's no school today! I want to come."

But he looked at me and said, "You're not ready. I don't

....

laid the bodies in caskets placed the dead bodies in long wooden boxes

pay their respects say goodbye

gave his services offered his help

have time to wait."

He left without me. That is why I am alive.

I was already involved in peace activities before my father was killed. Only six weeks earlier, I had been at a meeting of children and adults from all over Colombia where we had decided to create the Children's Movement for Peace. At that meeting I had talked as if I knew all about the war and its impact on children. I thought I understood because Aguachica, where I lived, **was in the thick of the conflict**. There were battles in the streets during the night. I was often woken up by gunfire. When I went to school in the morning, I saw the evidence—the blood on the sidewalks, the bullet-riddled buildings. And I had seen the victims at the **morgue**, not far from my father's office.

I had talked about this with confidence, as if I knew what the war meant—but when my father was murdered, I was **shattered not just by grief**, but because then I *understood* the war. I knew what it felt like to want to fight. I realized that no matter how much you want peace, you take a step towards violence when the war hits you personally.

This is the same trap that has caught so many people in my country.

The war has been going on all my life and all my parents' lives as well. Not many Colombians can remember a time when there wasn't war somewhere in the country. But it was not always as fierce as it is today, when so many armed groups are fighting one another—guerrilla organizations and

---

was in the thick of the conflict experienced the most fighting

morgue place where dead bodies are kept

shattered not just by grief very upset not just because of my sadness

paramilitary groups and the army. Some people say they are fighting for the poor, but the poor have suffered more than anyone else in the war. I think that some people are also fighting for revenge, or for power, or because they feel they have no other choice. Some young people join the armed groups because their families are poor and they see no other way out.

For many years, people in Aguachica managed to stay out of the war. People fled here to escape violence in other parts of the country. They came from all over Colombia, from the plains in the east, the coastal provinces of the north, and from the mountains that dramatically divide our country. For years, people from these different cultures lived quite happily in Aguachica, sharing their different festivals, foods, and games.

My brother Andrés was born in 1976 and I in 1981. In many ways, our early childhood was **idyllic and privileged**. We spent the week living in a huge rambling mansion in Aguachica town, where my father had his dental practice, but every weekend we went to our farm about ten miles away. My father loved it there. He was a dentist by profession, but in his heart he was a farmer.

The farm covered thirty-one acres and had two rivers running through it, one close behind the house, the other about half a mile away. The land was **rich and fertile**. We grew tomatoes, plantain, papaya, oranges, avocados, and other fruits in such abundance that we gave most of the harvest away. My father loved horses and from dawn to dusk he would be out riding or working with Hugo, the horse trainer.

As a child, I was quite ill with hepatitis and my parents

....

paramilitary groups groups of citizens with guns
idyllic and privileged perfect and special
rich and fertile very good for farming

were always protective of me, but Andrés was tough and **extroverted**. He had a passion for survival games. We "raided" the garden for bananas, sneaked oil from the kitchen, and cooked the bananas "Indian style" over burning rocks. We made bows and arrows, and hunted pigeons that we **plucked** and roasted ourselves. Sometimes we played barefoot soccer in the street, or cops and robbers, or guerrillas and soldiers. On hot days we plunged into the huge tank used for washing clothes, along with the dogs, some toads, and all our friends.

In 1989, my aunt moved into our house with her four children. Luche was the oldest cousin and my mother's goddaughter. They were always very close, more like mother and daughter. Even with so many people living there, the house in Aguachica never felt crowded. It was so enormous there were still some rooms we hardly used. The living room was so big we sometimes pushed back all the furniture to play indoor soccer!

Living as we do now, in a very **cramped** apartment and often afraid of what will happen next, the size of that house seems incredible to me. So does the freedom of the life we had then.

For me, becoming aware of the war was the same as growing up. It was always there but for a long time it seemed like something that happened to other people. In 1990, it was suddenly **right on our doorstep**.

When I was eight years old, a man was shot and killed not far from our house. I saw his body lying in the street. A few days later, my cousins and I were playing in our yard when a bomb exploded less than a block away. The noise was

....

extroverted very active

plucked took the feathers from

cramped crowded and small

right on our doorstep happening to us

deafening but none of us knew what it was. We stood there watching the bomb smoke **curl** into the air until our parents rushed out and pulled us into the house.

That year all our cattle were stolen, and men started showing up at the farm, demanding food, shelter, and money in return for their "protection" services. My father tried to turn them away but it was difficult. He paid one man **the equivalent of** about six thousand dollars in pesos just to leave us alone.

In December 1990, we had a Christmas party at the house in town and were singing carols when shooting started in the street outside. The next day, Andrés and I counted twenty-five holes in the walls of our house. On Christmas Day, we received a letter demanding payment of ten thousand dollars. A week later, another message gave instructions on how my mother was to go alone to a certain mango tree near a neighbor's property and leave the money there. A third letter warned that we had until January 12 to pay up, or we would **"face the consequences."**

My father told the police, who kept watch while my mother deposited the money as instructed. No one ever turned up to claim it.

A few weeks later, my mother realized she was being followed every time she left the house. Then her brother, who also lived in Aguachica, received an anonymous call warning that my mother should be "very careful." Finally, someone telephoned our house threatening to kidnap me. The caller even gave the name of the school I was attending, the Francisco

....

deafening so loud it hurt our ears
curl twist in circles as it went up
the equivalent of an amount that was equal to
face the consequences be punished

José de Caldas School, a small private school in a middle-class neighborhood of Aguachica.

My mother rushed to the school, grabbed me and my brother, and brought us home. The next day my family fled from Aguachica for the first time. My father **grudgingly** went with us. He thought my mother was overreacting. Yet within a week another dentist from Aguachica, Oswaldo Pajaro, was shot dead on an isolated dirt road near the town.

We never knew who had been **targeting** us or why. We could guess that it was because our land was fertile and someone else wanted it, or because someone didn't like my father's ideas. But we didn't really know *why*.

Most families displaced by the war are desperately poor and have nowhere to go. They move into camps or into overcrowded rooms on the edge of large towns and cities. In those days, my family was lucky since we still had money. We moved into a large, rented house in the pretty neighborhood of San Alonso in Bucaramanga, about eighty miles from Aguachica. I didn't mind Bucaramanga, but my father never liked it. He was an important man in Aguachica, but Bucaramanga had more than four hundred thousand people, and he was lost. He said it was easy for young people to **adapt and start over** but it was too late for him. He tried to **establish** a new dental practice but it never went well. Soon he was spending four days a week working in Aguachica.

In November 1994, after two years away, we went back to Aguachica, leaving Andrés in Bucaramanga to finish his

....

grudgingly reluctantly, bitterly

targeting trying to get

adapt and start over adjust and begin a new life

establish start

schooling. My father and I were especially happy to be home. He was confident that things were really beginning to improve, but my mother was still afraid. She says now, "What I feared most became reality."

My father never believed he would be killed because he said he had never done anything to hurt anyone. It seemed much more likely that one of us would be kidnapped, especially me. We discussed how I should behave if this happened. I was to be respectful to any kidnappers, to answer their questions politely, to never try to escape, and to **keep faith** that I would soon be freed.

I began attending José María Campo Serrano secondary school in a quiet **residential area on the outskirts** of Aguachica. Dogs and donkeys wandered loose along the hot, dusty road leading to the school, which was set among mango, guayaba, and almond trees. The school was like **an island of peace in the violent storm that raged in town**. Every week something terrible happened. One weekend, ten teenagers were killed by the police after they tried to kidnap a farmer. Then almost the entire population of a nearby village, Patiño, was massacred.

After a massacre, people sometimes went to the morgue to see if anyone they knew had been killed. I went inside, just once. It is not something I want to describe. I was not afraid. It was just so sad. Many of those who died were young and had been tortured. Many people gossiped about the dead, and about what they must have done to deserve such a terrible fate.

....

keep faith believe

residential area on the outskirts area where there were homes on the edge

an island of peace in the violent storm that raged in town a safe place in a very dangerous area

"Pueblo pequeno, infierno grande," my mother says now, which means "Small village, big hell."

Most people believed that the victims were guilty of something, but my brother and I realized this was not true when Edgar, a sixteen-year-old friend of ours, was tortured and murdered along with his uncle.

Towards the end of 1994, when I was thirteen years old, Luis Fernando Rincón was elected **mayor** of Aguachica and we were all hopeful that this would bring big changes. But days after Rincón took office, the director of the local hospital, Dr. José David Padilla, was murdered. Padilla was liked by many people and hundreds turned out to follow his coffin through the streets of Aguachica. A lot of us waved white handkerchiefs in protest against the raging violence. It seemed as if anyone who stood for peace and justice was at risk. They still are.

Soon afterwards, several armed groups informed Mayor Rincón that **he was on their death lists**. Rincón refused to be intimidated and instead announced that it was time for Aguachica to take a stand against the war. He called together leaders in the town—doctors, teachers, business people, and my father as well—to discuss the situation. They decided to hold a peace referendum. A referendum is when people are asked to vote on a particular question. Our referendum asked: Do you reject violence and agree to convert Aguachica into **a model municipality for peace**? That was the dream Rincón had; that Aguachica would set an example for Colombia, and show how a town that had been so violent, could become peaceful.

....

mayor leader

he was on their death lists they were going to kill him

a model municipality for peace an example of a peaceful city

The referendum was advertised on radio and television, in the newspapers and through public meetings and demonstrations. My father organized horseback rides for peace. More than forty of us, dressed in white, rode in **processions** through surrounding villages and Aguachica town. We were followed by the *papayera* who played folk music on wind instruments and drums, and by people carrying banners proclaiming Aguachica to be a "Model Municipality of Peace."

The whole **atmosphere** of Aguachica seemed to change and it certainly became less violent. More often I slept through the night, without being woken by gunfire.

....

processions a parade
atmosphere feeling, attitude

BEFORE YOU MOVE ON...

1. **Summarize** Reread pages 13–14. Who was fighting in the war? Who were the victims?

2. **Paraphrase** Reread pages 23–24. What did Juan Elias's mother mean when she said "small village, big hell"?

LOOK AHEAD Read pages 26–36 to see how some Colombian children came together to fight the war.

I talked about the referendum with some students at my school and we decided that young people should also be allowed to take part in the vote. Through my father, I already knew the mayor so I volunteered to ask him. The mayor agreed and with help from his office, we **launched** a youth campaign that involved all the schools and youth groups in the town. We held ecological walks, dances, and peace marches. Up to eight hundred children from poor and middle-class neighborhoods took part in a massive "camp-out for peace" run by the Scouts. Hundreds came to peace concerts held in the San Roque Park in central Aguachica, where I introduced performers and sometimes played my guitar and sang peace songs.

Colombia had never had a referendum like this one, so many journalists came from the capital to cover the story. Some asked me for interviews, and my mother became worried because I started getting a lot of attention. Several priests who had been helping the youth campaign had already been threatened and forced to leave the town. My mother begged me to be careful about anything I said in public, and especially never to **criticize anyone directly**.

Becoming well known meant that some of the other kids made fun of me. "Oh! Here comes the *pacifist*!" they would joke, "Here comes the *leader*."

None of it bothered me. My family believed it was important to care about the community and to do whatever we could to help. Even though I was only thirteen, I could see that the biggest problems facing us were violence and the war. Peace

....

launched started

criticize anyone directly say I did not like any one person or group

pacifist person who is against war

was needed more than anything else. Of course it is hard for a child to try to make peace but trying is the only way anything ever begins.

As the referendum grew closer, threats from the armed groups increased. Some of them announced that no one living in the mountain zones they controlled would be allowed to vote. They **denounced** the referendum as "no way to achieve peace" and said that all those who did vote would "have to suffer the consequences" because they would steal the list of voters and take their revenge.

On August 27, 1995, almost 10,400 adults and about 4,000 young people voted to support peace while fewer than 50 voted against. We thought it was a big success, yet close to seventy percent of Aguachicans did not vote at all. Fear had stopped a lot of people from going to the polls.

For a while the violence in Aguachica calmed down, but by the end of 1995, it was back again and just as fierce. More of those who had spoken out in favor of the referendum were forced to leave the town. Meanwhile, Mayor Rincón decided to **appoint** me as the Child Mayor of Aguachica, because of my work for peace. As the Child Mayor, I continued to visit schools to talk with students and teachers about creating a more peaceful and **tolerant learning atmosphere**. We held more youth concerts for peace and organized a competition to see who could write the best peace song.

In May, 1996, Mayor Rincón asked me if I would represent Aguachica at a workshop being organized by the United

....

denounced criticized

appoint choose, elect

tolerant learning atmosphere comfortable place where children can learn

Nations Children's Fund (UNICEF). On May 23, 1996, I traveled to the meeting at the **YMCA camp** at Santandercito, just outside Bogotá. There were twenty-seven children and thirty adults at the workshop, all of them involved in working for peace, human rights, or with children in some of the most violent municipalities in the country. Fifteen-year-old Farlis, the Child Mayor of Apartadó, was the oldest of the children. The youngest was nine-year-old Linía from Medellín. Other kids came from Cali, from the Guajira, from the Chocó, from Bogotá, and many other places. None of us really knew why we were there and that first evening we were very shy and uncertain, hardly talking at all.

The workshop began the next morning with each of the young people describing their lives and activities for peace. Almost everyone started by saying, "My home is very beautiful" or "I love my home." We all felt that way. We talked about the people, the food, the parties and music, the oceans, rivers, and mountains, the heat of the sun or the cool breezes. Then we described the bad things, the violence and the way it affected children. I was amazed to learn it was just as bad for others as it was for us in Aguachica. I had heard news reports of the violence but I had not *realized* **what it meant for** so many Colombian children.

We also learned about other countries affected by war. Nidya Quiroz, who had organized the meeting for UNICEF, showed us a film about Mozambique, a **war-torn country** in Africa. The film covered an election in which nearly seventy

....

YMCA camp center that provides activities for children
realized **what it meant for** *understood* how it affected
war-torn country country in war

thousand children had voted for their rights.

This led to a discussion of the rights of children. According to the law of almost every country in the world, children have a legal right to health, to food, to education, to play, to equality and nondiscrimination, to be protected from abuse, to express their opinions, to have access to information, and so on. In Colombia, of all places, we even had a right to peace! It was written in our **Constitution**, and it applied not just to children, but to everyone.

On the second day, we young people were asked to **recommend courses of action** to oppose violence and promote peace and our rights. It wasn't easy. We soon fell into arguments and some of the adults found it hard to keep quiet. They kept saying, "But have you thought about this . . ." or "What about that . . ." They seemed to be putting pressure on us when really we needed time to work things out at our own pace. Finally one of the children, I forget who, proposed a vote to ask all the adults to leave the room. **The motion was passed unanimously.** Only Cynthia de Windt, who had organized the games we played at the start of the workshop, stayed.

It took us a long time to sort out our ideas, but finally we were ready to invite the adults back in. We told them we wanted to create spaces where children's voices against the war could be heard, all over the country. We wanted cultural events where children could express their hopes and interest in peace through the arts. We wanted children all over Colombia to know about and understand their rights—and for parents and teachers to

....

Constitution country's official document of rights and beliefs

recommend courses of action suggest ways

The motion was passed unanimously. The suggestion was accepted by everyone.

understand the rights of children as well. Finally, we asked the adults in the meeting to work **as our partners** in making these things happen.

Children and adults began working together to turn these ideas into a plan of action. In the middle of the third day, the Children's Movement for Peace was **born**. This was to be a real movement of children, which no adults could join. They could only be our advisors. The first activity of the Children's Movement for Peace was going to be an election, just like the one held in Mozambique, in which Colombian children would choose which of their rights were most important to themselves and their communities. The election would draw attention to the effect of war on children, but it would also help children, teachers, and parents learn about child rights. Before leaving, all of us signed a **declaration** agreeing to support the Children's Movement for Peace and to promote the child rights election— which became known as the Children's **Mandate** for Peace and Rights.

I was so excited when I returned to Aguachica. A whole new way of seeing the future seemed to have opened up. I believed that if children from all over Colombia worked together we *could* change our country. Many people in Aguachica were discouraged by the renewed violence, but I kept talking about this new Children's Movement that was going to grow right across the country. I could see that what I was saying even gave some of the adults hope. They listened carefully and then, often they would say, "I want to help you, tell me what I can do."

....

as our partners together with us

born created

declaration written document

Mandate Command, Order

They trusted me.

So many lies have been told in my country for so many years that people do not know what or who to believe any more. They cannot always trust the newspapers, the radio or television, the politicians, the armed groups—but when they hear children talking about the violence and the way it affects us and how we want peace, somehow they know they are hearing the truth.

Four weeks after I returned to Aguachica, our horse trainer, Hugo, was murdered. Some armed men arrived at his house and set it on fire. As Hugo tried to rescue his daughter from the burning building, they grabbed him and forced his family to watch as they beat and tortured him. Hugo's fourteen-year-old nephew tried to stop the attackers. He ran forward shouting, "Stop! Please stop! Don't hurt him anymore!"

One of the armed men grabbed the boy and said, "So? You want some of this, too, do you? **You want some of this, too?**" And they shot him. They killed the child and then they killed Hugo.

The surviving family members **fled from** the farm and for a while stayed in Aguachica town. Then they had to run away again. I don't know where they are now. They have been displaced by the violence like so many millions in my country. As I am, too, now.

We always thought that Hugo's death and that of my father were connected, but to this day we have never been able to understand how.

....

You want some of this, too? Do you want to be hurt like your uncle?
fled from left

In the next couple of weeks there were several signs that our family was in danger. One morning, my father and Andrés were held up and threatened on their way to the farm. We received sinister anonymous telephone calls, including one that warned my mother to take care of me. She was told, "A man with a gun has been asking questions about what time Juan Elias gets out of school."

Right away my mother contacted the army base next to the school to ask for protection. They told her that three army **privates would be assigned as my bodyguards**, but they never showed up, so I did not go back to school.

About a week before the murder, my mother had a dream that she and the entire extended family were squeezed into my father's **Renault**. Everyone was there except him. We were traveling in a procession that was led by all the children. My cousin Luche, Andrés, and I were all dressed in white as if we were going to our first communion. Suddenly it began to pour, which was unusual. Aguachica is a very dry place. We rarely have big downpours.

My mother told my father about the dream, which she thought was a **premonition of death**, but my father never took such things seriously. He told her, "I am not ready to die yet."

The morning he was killed, we had just driven up from the farm. The morning was already hot. The palms framing the entrance to the townhouse were wilting in the heat. We learned that his office had been trying to reach him, because some patients were waiting. One was a regular client. The others,

....

privates would be assigned as my bodyguards soldiers would be chosen to protect me

Renault car

premonition of death warning that he would die

we now believe, were the **assassins**.

We stood in the entrance to the emergency room, my mother closer to the door, and I about fifteen feet away, talking with Alexander, one of the human rights workers from Aguachica. He had come to the hospital as soon as he heard about my father. While we waited for news, many more people showed up, all wanting to know if it was true. I told many of them, "Don't worry. He's going to be fine. They're taking care of him."

I really believed it. Right after my dad was shot he had **staggered** out of his office calling for help. "I'm all right," he'd told one of his neighbors, "but get help for Luche!"

There were so many people waiting outside the emergency room that I did not see that the doctor had come to talk to my mother. A school friend of Luche's overheard their conversation and came pushing through the crowd towards me. "Juan Elias, your father just died," he said.

I thought it was a very sick joke. "Don't mess with me," I told him. "My dad is fine." But then I looked across the room, saw my mother's face, and knew it was true. I rushed to her.

My mother is a strong woman, but I don't know **what it was that ran in her blood** that day. She had warned my father a thousand times about the danger he was in, but he wouldn't listen. Luche was still alive at that time but the doctor told us she needed a specialist's care. My mother found the strength from somewhere to call the army and try to get a helicopter to

....

assassins killers

staggered walked unsteadily

what it was that ran in her blood how she lived through

take Luche to the hospital in Bucaramanga. But the helicopter came too late, and so Luche was taken there in an ambulance. The journey took much longer than it should have because a landslide had virtually blocked the road. Eventually, the ambulance managed to cross the landslide, but Luche died on the outskirts of the city.

My brother Andrés was already in Bucaramanga where he attended the military academy. We called him and told him to come home because our father and Luche had been killed. All day I had been very controlled, but when Andrés walked into the house that evening, **it was as if a wall inside me broke down, and the flood rushed through**. I fell on my brother and wept like a baby. Since then, no one has seen me cry.

Nothing was the same afterwards. The house felt like a dead empty shell. The streets that were so familiar all looked strange. Nothing and nowhere felt safe. I thought all my work for peace was **worth nothing**, because it had not saved my father. The horrific violence that had engulfed our town had finally struck the heart of my family—and I had been unable to stop it.

I blamed myself. I asked myself, "What had I done that my father should die in such a violent way?"

During the funeral it poured with rain, just as it had in my mother's dream. More than fifteen hundred bouquets were sent to us. The route to the church and the church itself were packed. My father had given so much to our town. He was loved by so many people.

....

it was as if a wall inside me broke down, and the flood rushed through I could not stop myself from crying uncontrollably

worth nothing a waste of time

The threats against my family continued even after my father's death. Every time my mother, Andrés, or myself left the house, we were followed. It felt too dangerous for me even to walk around the corner. I always traveled by car. My friends stopped seeing me. Partly this was because of their own fear, but it was also my choice. I did not want to **endanger anyone**. Luche had been killed because she was with my father. I didn't want any of my friends to die just because they were with me.

I was frightened for myself and my family. I had only ever thought of how to make peace, not how to fight, but I was so afraid that I got a gun. I told myself that I would only use this gun **as an absolute last resort**, if I was in danger. But I was also angry. I thought, "If they try to kill me, at least I will **take some of them with me**."

One evening, about ten days after my father was killed, my family and my aunt's family were gathered together in an upstairs room. I went downstairs to get something from the kitchen. The lower floor was in darkness and through the living room windows that overlooked the garden, I suddenly saw a shadow of a man. I ducked behind a pillar in the living room and watched him as he crept through the bushes. He was looking at the lighted windows upstairs. I could see the shape of a gun in his hand.

I realized that I could get my gun and kill this man. I could shoot him before he knew what had **hit him**. It would be revenge for my father's death. I would be protecting my family. And almost no one in Colombia would blame me for shooting

....

endanger anyone put others in danger
as an absolute last resort if I had no other choice
take some of them with me kill some of them also
hit him happened

him—violent revenge is the expected reaction of any young man who loses his father the way I lost mine. Yet while all of this was true, I did nothing.

My father had always wanted me to work for peace. How could I become violent now? The only way I could show respect and love for my father, the only way I could help to save my family, was by trying to make peace. The only way I could help **ensure** that no other child would suffer the way I had, was by trying to make peace. Killing him would bring no peace to me, or my family, or my country. In fact, by killing him I would lose everything. I would be no better than he was.

I watched him and then, for no clear reason, he turned and walked away. Not long afterwards I got rid of the gun and have never had one since. Two months later, I went to Bogotá to take part in the first meetings of the Children's Movement for Peace. With all the grief I was feeling, it **was a blessing to be able to throw myself into** the Movement.

....

ensure make sure
was a blessing to be able to throw myself into really helped to work hard for

BEFORE YOU MOVE ON...

1. **Sequence** Reread pages 27–29. How was the Children's Movement for Peace formed?

2. **Author's Bias** Reread pages 35–36. Juan Elias's father was killed. How did this affect his view of violence?

THE LINE BETWEEN NOW AND TOMORROW

When my cousin "Enrique" was seventeen, his girlfriend got pregnant. There was pressure to marry and he wanted to **do the "right thing"** anyway. He'd never attended school regularly and wasn't working at the time, but he went looking for a job to **support** his new wife and baby. He'd always dreamed of being a car mechanic but no one would **take him on**. He tried factories, shops, construction sites, and hotels. He tried all over our town of Apartadó, but he couldn't find a thing.

Eventually he decided he would have to join one of the armed groups. Some of the armed groups pay quite well, but the work is lousy. The work is all about killing.

Enrique and I are the same age, and for years we have been very close. He is like my brother. When I heard that he was going to join one of these groups, I rushed over to his house and **confronted** him. He was in the tiny living room, stretched out in front of the television. I don't think I even said hello.

"How could you do this? How! I don't believe it!"

"Man, Farlis, I don't have no choice."

"You've always got a choice. There's always a choice, man!"

"I can't see it. There's nothing there for me. I tried everywhere. How am I going to support my child?"

....

do the "right thing" help the mother of his child
support help pay for the expenses of
take him on hire him
confronted talked to; questioned

"You think *that* is the way to support a family? What kind of father would that make you? You call that a job!"

He looked away. "I don't have no choice," he said quietly.

"How can you even think of it!"

Did he think he would be able to kill? Would he be able to **open fire on** women and children and old people?

Certainly the men in those armed groups had money and power. They wore good clothes and expensive sunglasses. A poor young boy might easily think of it as a good opportunity but only if he didn't think about the consequences.

"**It doesn't come without a price**," I told him. "There's a price to pay even inside this family."

He didn't look at me. He didn't speak.

"You listen to me. If you join up with them, then you can say goodbye to me right now because you won't ever see me again, or if you do, then I won't know you, you understand? Not only that, you won't ever see anyone in my family again. None of us. We won't see you. We won't talk to you. We won't know you."

I felt like crying. I loved Enrique but he couldn't do this!

He still didn't look at me.

"You join up and that's the last you'll see of us," I said once more, and left.

A few days later I heard that he had changed his mind. Eventually he found employment on one of the banana **plantations**. It was low-paying and hard work, but it was peaceful.

....

open fire on shoot bullets at

It doesn't come without a price Joining an armed group is going to change everything

plantations farms

I started working for peace when I was fifteen years old. By then I knew that this war is our war, it is my war. It does not belong to someone else, it belongs to me, to all Colombians. That is why I could not stand by and watch Enrique do this terrible thing.

The war has lasted so long because we have always waited for other people to make peace—yet no one else can do it for us. We must make peace ourselves. We cannot let **another generation of Colombians grow up in the midst** of war.

For fourteen years I lived on a banana plantation about ten miles from Apartadó, in the northwest region of Colombia known as Urabá. My father worked on the plantation, harvesting and packing bananas. My mother ran a small business from our home, selling soft drinks and snacks to the workers. We lived in a small adobe house with a tin roof in a dusty **compound** shaded by mango and guayaba trees. There were four kids in our family. I was the oldest, then came my brother Obier and sisters Elis and Yeleny.

We grew up rough, like other farm kids, playing in the fields and swimming in the tank where they washed the bananas. We traveled to school hanging on to the back of a banana truck, bouncing over the rough roads, the air filled with the sweet scent of the fruit. It was hot and dusty and it didn't matter how **much care we took** before leaving home—by the time we got to school in Nuevo Colonía we always looked like farm kids.

....

another generation of Colombians grow up in the midst Colombian children live in the middle

compound yard

much care we took clean we were

Surviving in school meant being loyal to your friends and not being a *sapo*. *Sapo* literally means "toad" but it is also slang for an informer or a tattletale. We forced *sapos* to transfer to another class by ignoring them. It was harsh but it **was also a reflection of the world outside**. *Sapos* can get people killed in Colombia. Yet being unable to speak the truth—and sometimes all a *sapo* is doing is telling the truth—is a big problem, too. There might be a massacre in the middle of a town in broad daylight, but no one will admit to seeing anything. They will whisper the truth to one another, but they won't tell the authorities. They are too afraid.

When I was eleven, **I was given the silent treatment myself**, not because I'd been a *sapo*, but because I refused to take sides in an argument. A group of my friends had accused a girl in our class of stealing money and a huge conflict erupted. You had to be either for this girl or against her, and all my friends were against her. Everyone assumed I would stand by them, but there was no evidence that the girl was a thief. I couldn't be sure. I didn't want to oppose my friends, though, so I just said nothing. Everyone got mad and, for a whole year, no one spoke to me.

Around that time, my only friend and the only one (I thought) who understood me, was a boy who worked on the plantation. We can call him "Alfredo."

The other farm girls teased me about him. They said, "You better watch out for that Alfredo, Farlis! You watch out girl because that boy is a *guerrillero*!" (a member of a **left-wing** armed group).

....

was also a reflection of the world outside showed how people acted outside our school

I was given the silent treatment myself none of my classmates would speak to me

left-wing radical

I knew some people around the plantation were involved in the war, but I never thought that about Alfredo. He was too sweet and gentle. I thought the other girls were jealous because he was so good-looking.

Alfredo and I would walk for hours around the plantation, holding hands and talking about the future. I lay in bed at night imagining how Alfredo and I would marry and live together in Apartadó with our many children. But one day I walked into our house and found him there, cleaning his gun. He had come to buy something from my mother and, while waiting, had taken out his gun, and started to work on it. When I walked in, he gave me a smile, as if he were doing nothing out of the ordinary.

I have always hated violence, hated guns, hated the war. Alfredo tried to make excuses, the way people like that do, but I told him right away **it was over between us**.

"I don't want this kind of life for myself or for my children," I said. I was so young it seems like a joke now, but I felt **like my world was breaking in two**.

Soon afterwards, Alfredo left the farm, but I was **heartbroken**. I couldn't sleep, my schoolwork suffered, and my mother was furious over my falling grades. I didn't know how to explain.

Finally my Spanish teacher, Señor Rodrigues, asked if I would like to "talk things over." We went to a small café in Nuevo Colonía, and over some strong Colombian coffee, I spilled the whole story of Alfredo, the gun, the silence of my friends, the teasing of the farm girls, my embarrassment, and

....

it was over between us that I did not want to see him anymore

like my world was breaking in two very upset and confused

heartbroken very sad and hurt

broken heart. He seemed to understand everything. He didn't laugh at me or make me feel young and ridiculous. He treated me like an adult.

"You must understand," he told me, "that you hold your own future in your own hands. Your future does not belong to anyone else, not to your parents, and especially not to this boy. It is yours and you can make of it anything you want."

After that, I didn't think of Señor Rodrigues as just my Spanish teacher, but as *mi professor de alma*, the teacher of my soul.

One morning, when I was thirteen years old, my mother woke us up and told us that more than thirty people had been killed during an outdoor party in the old *barrio*, (neighborhood) of La Chinita in Apartadó. My grandmother, aunts, uncles, and cousins lived in *barrios* not far from La Chinita.

"They will all be fine," my mother told us. "I'll go there and see, but they will all be fine." **Yet there was fear in her eyes.**

She went first to my aunt's house, then to my grandmother's, and then to La Chinita and **the site of the massacre.** The bodies were still lying in the street, their faces covered with cloths. People walked among them, lifting the cloths to see if anyone they knew had been killed. My family was safe, but a friend of my mother's was among the dead, and my mother heard the story of how it had happened from one of the survivors.

There had been a party in the **small plaza to raise funds** for a local school. It was a beautiful evening and many people

....

Yet there was fear in her eyes. But she was scared.

the site of the massacre the place where the killings happened

small plaza to raise funds town's center to earn money

came out, young and old, to dance and have fun under the stars. Some of the people at the party **were former** members of one of the armed groups. Apparently they were the target of the attack, though most of the people who died were not connected with any armed group.

Around eleven at night, the party was in full swing when a truck full of masked, armed men drove into the square. They jumped from the vehicle and opened fire. They didn't seem to care who they hit. Old people and children were among the thirty-five people who died.

One of the men had drawn his gun on the husband of my mother's friend.

"Please don't kill him," she had pleaded. "Please, for the sake of our children, I beg you!"

But he killed them both.

After the massacre at La Chinita, the violence in and around Apartadó became much more intense. Armed groups sometimes turned up in villages, forced all the men, women, and children into the plaza, and sifted through them, **executing anyone found guilty of supporting their rivals**. They murdered grocers who sold food to the "wrong" side. They killed teachers who were teaching the "wrong" lessons. They slaughtered husbands in front of wives, parents in front of children, community leaders in front of entire villages. Many families were ordered to abandon their homes. Money was **extorted** from those they allowed to remain.

They sometimes showed up at farms like ours, gathered

....

were former used to be

executing anyone found guilty of supporting their rivals killing anyone that they thought was helping their enemies

extorted forcefully taken

all the workers together, called out the names of supposed **"subversives"** and killed them. They also assassinated petty thieves and other delinquents, claiming that they were "cleaning up" the town. In the space of three years, more than twelve hundred people in Apartadó were assassinated, including seventeen members of the local government. Almost no one was arrested or **brought to trial** for these murders.

One of the worst massacres came in September 1995. A bus carrying workers from Apartadó to one of the plantations was forced off the road at a place called Bajo del Oso. They took the passengers off the bus, tied their hands, threw them face down in the mud, and opened fire. Twenty-five people died, including a fourteen-year-old boy. The few that survived only did so because they were protected by the bodies of the dead.

A friend of my father's was killed on that bus. We never spoke about it as a family, but we all sensed that next time it could be one of us. If my father was late coming home from work, we were all afraid but there was nothing we could do—or so I thought.

When I was fourteen, I began attending the José Celestino Mutis High School in Apartadó. During the week, I stayed with my aunt in the town. After the quietness and isolation of the plantation, I loved the energy of the town. Newspaper stories of Apartadó made it seem like everyone was **allied** with one armed group or another, **perpetually plotting war** or carrying out hideous acts of violence. In fact, most people were never

....

"subversives" enemies of their group
brought to trial judged in court
allied united, working
perpetually plotting war always planning battles

involved in the violence, except sometimes as its victims, and the violence wasn't continuous either. Most nights, the small bars of Apartadó blasted loud music, and people strolled the streets around the central park or sat at tables in sidewalk cafés.

I walked to school every day along the avenue beside the hospital. Teak trees grew close together along the roadside, their branches arching high over the road. Partway along this avenue was Don Fermin's fruit stall with its rich fragrances of papaya, mamocilla, mango, and banana. Don Fermin always **called out a greeting** as I passed, and if I missed a day at school he noticed and wanted to know the reason why. Many people in Apartadó were like him. They were sweet and caring and just happened to live in the middle of a war.

Celestino was tougher than my previous school, with a lot of fights, petty theft, and drug abuse. Our ninth-grade class was considered to be the most disruptive in the school, but we were proud of this. We challenged our teachers and objected to the entire education system in Colombia, which favored the rich and privileged. We demanded more participation in deciding what and how we would learn. We **verbally abused teachers who were inadequate, and I was often the ringleader of** these attacks. I thought the school owed us a decent education. I thought that teachers who could not do their job properly had no business standing in front of the class. My desperation over my education grew as I grew. My parents were too poor to send me to university. I knew that whatever I learned at Celestino could determine my future.

....

called out a greeting said hello

verbally abused teachers who were inadequate, and I was often the ringleader of yelled at bad teachers, and I usually started

My mother kept telling me not to worry. She promised everything would turn out well if I **stayed true to my ideals**. I love my mother very much and believe she is one of the wisest people in the world—but on this subject I thought she was crazy.

....

stayed true to my ideals did not forget my beliefs

BEFORE YOU MOVE ON...

1. **Cause and Effect** What could happen to someone who was a "sapo" in Colombia? Reread page 40.

2. **Assumption** What did Farlis assume about Alberto? How did she find out she might be wrong?

LOOK AHEAD Read pages 47–56 to learn how Farlis made peace between two communities.

In 1996, when I was fifteen years old, one of my friends slipped my name onto the ballot for class representative. I won that election and when all the student representatives got together, I was elected as the president of the student government. Then in April, 1996, Gloria Cuartas, the mayor of Apartadó, invited several hundred student leaders to a special meeting. She told us that Graça Machel was going to visit Apartadó to learn about the effects of war on children.

These days, Graça Machel is better known as the wife of Nelson Mandela, but in 1996 she was studying the **impact of armed conflict** on children for the United Nations. For months she had been traveling from conflict to conflict, interviewing hundreds of people and gathering information for her report.

To prepare for her visit to Apartadó, more than five thousand children became involved in a Week of **Reflection**, which was supported by the Catholic Church, the Colombian Red Cross, and the United Nations Children's Fund (UNICEF). We wrote letters, poems, and stories; we painted pictures; and our work was posted on walls in the town hall.

One eleven-year-old girl wrote, "We know how to write the word 'peace' because our teachers have taught us which letters to use, but we do not know what it really means. It must be very beautiful."

Another child wrote an anonymous letter: "Dear Graça Machel, my father was **the world** to me, but since he was killed I cannot rest. I used to be a good student but now I only disappoint my mother. She tries to help but we

....

impact of armed conflict effect of wars
Reflection Thinking
the world very important

live in the shadows, under a great weight of sadness."

The drawings were about the terrible violence of our lives. One picture entitled "My House" showed a simple dwelling, with a dead body lying in the foreground and presumably the family members gathered around.

"Violence in Urabá is stupid," wrote another child, "because we kill each other over stupid things. As the saying goes, *por ver caer*, to see is to die." He meant that if you witnessed a killing in Urabá, you were **as good as dead yourself**.

During that week, a hundred student representatives were divided into commissions to discuss different aspects of the conflict. There was a commission for peace, a commission for human rights, another for displaced people, and so on. We met in one vast hall in the Colegio Pueblo Nuevo in central Apartadó.

I was inspired by discussing and analyzing what had been happening to us, and by the idea that the views of children mattered. I remember telling our group in the Peace Commission, "People in Colombia would rather fight over a disagreement than talk about it. If they do talk, they are only interested in proving the other person wrong, not in finding **common ground**. But how can we learn to be peaceful if we don't understand what it means? No one here has ever lived in peace. We have been fighting from the time we were born and so have our parents."

By the end of the week we had plenty of ideas. We wanted peace education in our schools and a youth movement that

....

live in the shadows, under a great weight of sadness cannot escape the pain of my father's death

as good as dead yourself probably going to be killed, too

common ground something they share

worked for peace. We had also drawn up the Declaration of the Children of Apartadó, which asked the armed groups to stop killing our parents and to make the streets safe for us to play. We said that none of the armed groups had a role to play in the future of Apartadó but that the young people had a big role because we are the future.

Some towns in Colombia have Child Mayors who act as spokespeople for children. On the last day, I was elected the first Child Mayor of Apartadó. My first task was to present our Declaration to Graça Machel. I was fifteen years old.

The town hall was **packed** for her visit but I lost all fear when I went to the microphone. I said that people in Apartadó had been trying to forget the violence. They did not want to remember the terrible events of the war. Yet I was sure that for those who lost family members in massacres, like those of La Chinita and El Bajo del Oso, the pain would never die.

"If you kill the father, you always kill a part of his children as well," I said.

Then I read the Declaration aloud and presented it to Graça Machel. She promised she would **carry our voices** to the United Nations so that leaders from around the world would understand what the war was doing to us.

Things might have ended there but they didn't. We were inspired by that week. I was the Child Mayor and other students including Johemir had also been elected to positions in a local government of children. We thought other students should know about their government and participate in it, so

....

packed full of people
carry our voices tell our story

we sent out notices to all the schools inviting everyone to attend a meeting.

Truthfully, I thought that being the Child Mayor was a bit ridiculous. What could I really do? I had no power. I had no expectations about the first meeting either, but more than one hundred children showed up. When they kept on coming, to two or three meetings a week, I began to realize that we had really started something.

Most of us were between nine and fifteen years old. We met in parks or on soccer grounds, a rowdy mass of kids **who argued ferociously about** what we could and could not do to promote peace. We knew that ending poverty could help to end the war, but we could do nothing about that. We knew that reducing unemployment would help, but we could do nothing about that either. We could not stop the bullets and the **machetes**. We could not end the violence. But we believed we could begin to build peace among ourselves.

My aunt lived in the *barrio* of Obrero and for several months that community had been feuding with the nearby *barrio* of Policarpa. It was difficult for young people from the two *barrios* to even walk through one another's territory. We planned a peace carnival for kids from these two communities where they could play together and see how much they had in common. With help from the Church, some of us visited parents in the two communities to explain the event. It was held **on neutral ground**, with water games and soccer, face painting, clowns, music, and more. Nothing like it had been seen in Apartadó

....

who argued ferociously about who passionately discussed
machetes knives
on neutral ground in an area where there was no fighting

before. It was a success but once was not enough. We planned more for the future.

We also organized youth clubs where the students could play music, basketball, and volleyball, or simply hang out after school. Yet any gathering of young people in Apartadó could be mistaken for a **recruitment exercise** for one of the armed groups. Just a suspicion like that could lead to violence, or even a massacre. As the Child Mayor, I decided I should explain what we were doing to the commander of the most powerful armed group in the town.

Through another student, I arranged to meet the commander—we can call him "Perez"—in a small café. He was a good-looking man, about twenty-six years old. He bought me a soda and seemed charming and interested while I explained that the school clubs would be "**genuine** youth activities." I told him that children in Apartadó needed to fill their minds and that this would help to take their thoughts away from the violence.

Perez told me these ideas were interesting. "We are here so that things will improve. I would rather young people were busy enjoying themselves than out joining the rebels or killing someone."

I had wanted to keep my meeting with Perez a secret because I was afraid people would think I **was a sympathizer**, but just talking with him established a connection between us. Afterwards, if I was in the street and he was passing, he stopped to talk. I was walking home from school with a group of friends

....

recruitment exercise way to get new soldiers
genuine actual, real
was a sympathizer agreed with Perez's ideas

one day, and Perez drove up with a truckload of armed men. He called me over and I couldn't ignore him.

My mother had told me that in life it is often ~~necessary to~~ **be like a chameleon**.

"Sometimes you must appear to be red even though you are green, but no matter what, you must always **stay true to the essence of the creature that you really are**."

I thought that in dealing with Perez I had to be a chameleon. I always kept my distance, but I had to get along with him, because it was too dangerous to be his enemy. Not everyone understood.

Then Perez dropped by to speak with my mother. She was at home on the plantation doing the family washing in a large cement sink on the back porch. Perez bought a soft drink and sat on a wooden bench nearby, chatting casually while she continued with the laundry.

He mentioned he had seen me on television and read stories about me in the newspapers. "So Farlis is becoming famous," he laughed. "What's all this about her becoming the Child Mayor of Apartadó? What does that mean?"

"It doesn't mean anything," my mother told him, "it's just something the children came up with. Children's rights. That sort of thing."

"Does she get paid for it then?" asked Perez.

"No, they're just kids. They don't get paid."

"She's young to get **mixed up in politics**," said Perez. "Doesn't it worry you?"

....

be like a chameleon change your appearance

stay true to the essence of the creature that you really are be yourself

mixed up in politics involved in government

"It's not politics," my mother said. "It's the Church and the Red Cross. It's like a club."

My mother thought nothing of that visit from Perez, but it worried me. I knew that working for peace could be dangerous, and I was sensitive to anything that was out of the ordinary. Sometimes just the fear that anything bad could happen, especially to my family, made me weep and feel like running away from the peace movement. Yet the other kids were depending on me, and, in a way, I felt that my own unborn children were depending on me, too. I could not turn away, no matter how afraid I was. I could only be careful and try to stay safe.

Once a journalist tried to trick me into saying something dangerous about one of the armed groups, just so he could get a story. He would have **sacrificed me** for that. I learned never to accuse anyone of anything—I would always describe **atrocities** and **denounce the violence**, but I never talked about who was responsible. I simply said I did not know. This became a way for all the young people in the peace movement to protect themselves.

A month after Graça Machel's visit, the Children's Movement for Peace in Colombia was born during a workshop at Santandercito, just outside Bogotá. I returned from that meeting full of enthusiasm. At the next gathering of the Apartadó movement, I told the kids, "Listen, we are going to make **the whole of** Colombia sit up and listen to us. There is

....

sacrificed me risked my life
atrocities awful occurrences
denounce the violence say the violence was terrible
the whole of everyone in

going to be a special election for children called the Children's Mandate in which we will choose the rights that are most important to us. We have to make sure that every single child in Apartadó understands their rights and takes part in this vote. If we succeed, then even the President, all the armed groups, and every adult in Colombia will have to listen."

It was a huge **vision**, this idea of making everyone listen to children. People were afraid for us. Some said that if children went to the polls to vote, they would become targets of the armed groups. For years every election in Colombia had been disrupted by violence. Eventually, even Cecilio Adorna, who led the UNICEF office in Bogotá, also began to have doubts.

UNICEF and a local peace organization called Redepaz were the main **sponsors** of the Children's Mandate. They had the **backing** of many other organizations and about twenty young people like myself were advising on how to make it a success. Sometimes UNICEF flew me to Bogotá to take part in workshops and meetings. On one of these trips, I heard that Señor Adorna was thinking of canceling the entire election. Right away I went to his office and **hovered beside** his open door.

He looked up from his desk. "Farlis?"

"How can you do this to us?"

"Come in," he said. "Sit down."

I sat and repeated myself. "How can you do this to us?"

"I am only thinking of your safety. The election could be very dangerous. They might harm you."

....

vision dream
sponsors supporters
backing support
hovered beside stood near

"But how can you disappoint so many children? They are looking forward to this. We have been working towards it for months."

"But what if a child is hurt? What then?"

"We have to take our chances. We can't let fear stop us. We have to trust that they will leave us to vote in peace."

I left it with him like that, and he spent a night thinking it over. The next day, the date of the Children's Mandate was set for October 25, 1996.

With UNICEF and Redepaz, we wrote to the armed groups asking for peace on the day of our vote. Some of them even wrote back and told us they would respect our rights. One group even wrote about the rights of their own children and about wanting to **forge links** between us.

The day of the vote came, and for the first time in our memory there was peace, if only for a day, in Colombia. No child was hurt or even threatened. We had hoped that maybe 500,000 young people would take part, but more than 2.7 million children and adolescents **turned up at** the polls. In some of the most violent towns, like Apartadó, almost every single person between the ages of seven and eighteen took part in the vote. Everywhere, children chose the right to life and the right to peace as the most important for themselves and their communities, and the most abused in Colombia.

I read the story of our election on the front page of our country's largest newspaper, *El Tiempo*. We were only children. We had no power, but we were making our country sit up and

....

forge links create bonds
turned up at came to
El Tiempo *The Times* (in Spanish)

listen to us, because our ideas about the war and about the need for peace were important. I was amazed and happy and yet I knew it was only the beginning. **A long struggle lay ahead.**

A long struggle lay ahead. We were going to have to fight for what we believed in.

BEFORE YOU MOVE ON...

1. **Problem and Solution** How did Farlis try to stop the fighting between Obrero and Policarpa?

2. **Simile** Reread page 52. What did Farlis's mother mean when she told Farlis to "be like a chameleon"?

Beto – 16

FALLING IN LOVE WITH LIFE

Eighteen months ago my eldest brother "Fredy" showed up at our house in La Libertad, a poor community in Medellín. It was the middle of the night. **He was drugged out of his mind and in deep distress.** "They're going to kill me," he was murmuring. "I know they are going to kill me."

He wouldn't tell us what had happened, but there had been an argument between him and a gang in our neighborhood and now they were out to get him. He seemed full of grief and regret, as well as fear, that **his days were numbered**. He wanted to roll back time and make it better. He came to us because there was nowhere else to go, but he knew they would come looking for him at our house. He left that night, and although we sometimes hear news of him, we haven't seen him since.

Fredy is my brother, but he's like a stranger to me. When he was a baby, my mother used to leave him with a friend of hers while she went to work. One day this "friend"—we can call her "Gloria"—told my mother that she wasn't going to give Fredy back. My mother begged and pleaded with Gloria and her family but they insulted her and told her she wasn't fit to be a mother. The police got involved, but they didn't do anything. My mother tried to discuss things calmly, but Gloria's husband

---

He was drugged out of his mind and in deep distress. He had taken too many drugs and was very upset.

his days were numbered he was going to die soon

attacked her with a machete.

She didn't see Fredy again until three years ago. By then he was twenty-seven years old and **messed up**, into gangs, and taking drugs. He had a young daughter, but he didn't treat her right. Some days he gave her everything she wanted. Other days he **whipped** her. He had no control over himself.

My mother lost Fredy long before I was born, and I know it must have affected her badly. Maybe that was when she began to have a problem with alcohol. She never managed money well either. She had other children, some with one man and then with my father, but both of these men abandoned her. My older brothers and sisters did nothing to help. As they grew older, they started **dragging her down**. Everyone piled criticism on her, on each other, and on me as well.

I am the youngest in our family and for a long time I was at the bottom of this heap of suffering and violence. A lot of kids living in families like mine end up joining a gang or even fighting in the war. Most are looking for a way out of the pain they suffer at home, but they end up with something that is much worse. I managed to escape that fate, because, despite all the sadness and violence in my home, I grew up feeling that I could get through it all and make a good life. I know my mother has problems, but I love and respect her. At last she is a good friend to me—but it wasn't always that way.

After she lost Fredy, my mother brought "Germán" to live in our house. I don't know where she found him, but she adored

....

messed up in trouble

whipped hit, beat

dragging her down making her feel bad

him as if he were her own son. He was nine when I was born and was **a menace** to me when I was growing up. He always made me feel uneasy and insecure, and sometimes he hurt me. As a teenager he began stealing, first from us, and then from the neighbors. Eventually he was caught, and when I was about eight years old, Germán was sent to Bella Vista jail.

For a few years life was fine for us, but when I was ten, Germán came back. Prison had made him much worse and my life became a nightmare. He beat, **tormented, and terrorized** my sister Milena and me. We were never safe at home alone with him, but we didn't tell our mother what was happening. Germán threatened to beat us if we told, and my mother seemed to love him so much, that for a long time I didn't know if she would believe us.

At school I became a pest. I did anything to cause trouble. I messed around with cockroaches, shoved them in kids' faces. I called everyone names. The teacher with stuck-out teeth was "Crazy Fang." The math teacher's first name was Guillermo but I called him *"guerrillermo"* because it sounded like *"guerilla."* I talked in class, made silly noises that got everyone **snickering**, dropped books, or suddenly laughed out loud for no reason. I didn't care if a teacher or student was talking—I did anything to disrupt the class.

When my mother beat me, which happened often in those days, I screamed **my lungs out**. Afterwards I wrote messages to myself in a secret notebook—dramatic statements like:

"I am going to leave home! I know I can get on in life!"

....

a menace an annoyance
tormented, and terrorized tortured, and frightened
snickering laughing, giggling
my lungs out very loudly

Although I was so miserable at home and school, I always believed that someday everything would be okay. I don't know why, but I am known to be stubborn. Once I get an idea I can hold onto it no matter what anyone says or does. I knew that running away wasn't the answer to my problems. Life was even tougher on the streets.

I found other ways to escape. Around that time a cartoon series called *Zodiac Knights* was playing on television. I played **solitary fantasy games** based on the show and always took the part of the heroic swan. The swan had fabulous feathers, bronze armor, and it moved with a powerful grace. Like him, I possessed incredible powers that I had **acquired** at the North Pole—the diamond dust that froze my enemies to death—and I defended Athens from the forces of evil. The swan's mother had died during a terrible shipwreck. In one dramatic game, I was about to be killed, but, like the swan, I took out a rosary that my mother had given me, and thanked the gods for giving me such a wonderful mother. Because of that prayer, the **Cosmic Forces** gave me strength to win the battle.

In the show, when the swan wanted to visit his mother's tomb, he had to crack the ice and dive into the depths of the cold, dark sea. I used to think, "I would do that for my mother."

But it was the Church that really **gave me a way out of** the violence at home. While Germán was in prison, I had become an altar boy at the church of San Francisco de Assisi that lies on the border of the *barrios* of La Libertad and Caicedo. It was by far the grandest building in our community, soaring

....

solitary fantasy games pretend games by myself

acquired received

Cosmic Forces Powerful Spirits

gave me a way out of let me get away from

over the small cement houses, with a high arched doorway and a towering spire. Inside it was cool and dark. Light filtered through the narrow windows and lay in stripes across the pews, the altar, and the confession booths.

Ever since my first communion I had loved the rituals and the activity of the church. As an altar boy, I helped the priests, handling the tray of wafers and the chalice during communion. I liked being part of the drama and the holiness of the place. The priests were also good to me, especially the Spanish priest called Manolo. He **opened up a new world of ideas for me** and always had time to listen, to talk, and to ask about my family. I worked hard to **win his approval** and to become the finest altar boy in the parish. Soon I was serving at every morning mass, as well as the Sunday evening mass.

By 1996, I was twelve years old and looking for every opportunity to get away from Germán. Through the church, I joined a theater and dance group that put on shows in the *barrio*. And through this group I heard about a workshop on community leadership. I went along thinking it would be for young people, but I turned out to be the only kid there. I didn't care. I hung around because I'm always curious and wanted to know what they were up to.

I **just about fell over** when they began to discuss violence in the home. It seems crazy but I never knew that people talked about things like that. I thought, "*¡¡Ave María!!*" because it was like coming to a place where people really understood what was happening to me.

....

opened up a new world of ideas for me taught me to think in ways I never imagined

win his approval get him to like me

just about fell over could not believe it

I thought, "This is exactly what I have been looking for!" because these people also talked about how we could change things for ourselves. **It was like the perfect glove slipping onto my hand!** It never bothered me that I was only twelve and they were adults. I never thought, "Oh I can't do this because I am too young." I understood everything they were saying and knew right away that I could also be a community leader.

The workshop was run by an organization called Corporación Regional. Over the next few months I went to many more of their training sessions, and often I was the youngest in the room by almost a decade. They liked me coming along. I was like their mascot. And, because of those sessions, I began to understand my mother better. I began to understand my own behavior at school better. Most of all I realized that I did not have to be a victim. Germán was still beating me up sometimes, but I finally realized that what he was doing to me was not my fault. I knew I could **overcome** it and help other people do the same.

I tried to help Maritza, who was also an altar girl at San Francisco de Assis. At first she wouldn't listen to me. She cursed me and said some terrible things. It was hard, but I never let it stop me. Eventually we were able to **close the gap between us**, and to work together first through the church and then with kids in the community.

In June 1996, Alberto, who was one of the organizers of the Corporación Regional, called me urgently to the office. He introduced me to Oscar, who worked with the peace network

....

It was like the perfect glove slipping onto my hand! This group was exactly what I needed!

overcome beat; rise above

close the gap between us become friends

called Redepaz. They were both very excited. Oscar told me, "There's going to be this amazing election for children about their rights! A Children's Movement for Peace has been formed! We've examined all our records and we've figured out that you should be the *procuradorcito* of Antioquia! It's great, huh?"

I wasn't sure it was so great. A *"procurador"* is a lawyer or a **solicitor** who is concerned with civil law. *"Procuradorcito"* means "little lawyer" and Antioquia is the name of our province; a huge place with millions of people. Oscar was telling me that I should be the "little lawyer" of this huge province? It seemed ridiculous. Then Oscar introduced me to a boy called Gustavo Adolfo who he said was the *"alcaldecito"* ("little mayor"), to Harry who was the *"personerito"* ("little representative"), and a girl called Diana who was the designated *"consejerita"* ("little counselor."). He told us that the Children's Movement had the backing of some big organizations, and the first activity would be a child rights election called the Children's Mandate. The next day we went on local television to explain all this to other young people.

At first I was confused and thought they were **manipulating** me, but it began to make sense after we began teaching other kids about their rights. I worked in several schools in my own and other *barrios*. Groups of us ran recreational, theatrical, and artistic events to motivate the children to take part in the vote. Meanwhile, groups of *"semilleros"* (or "seedbeds" for peace) **sprang up all over the city**. These were groups of children connected with the church or with human rights organizations;

....

solicitor representative, advisor

manipulating tricking, misleading

sprang up all over the city started forming in many areas of the city

they worked together to promote child rights and peace in their communities.

On the day of the Mandate, I went to the Campo Valdéz school to **cast my vote**, and chose the right to life. Afterwards, an argument **broke out** among several of us about which right was most important. Harry had chosen the right to peace because he said there was no point in having a right to life if you couldn't live in peace. Gustavo Adolfo had chosen the right to **justice** because he said the lack of justice was the main reason for the war.

But I told them, "What's the point in having a right to peace or a right to justice if you're dead?"

I thought it was great that we had that kind of discussion. It showed how seriously we took the election.

The turnout in Medellín was enormous. Almost every **eligible child voted**. Afterwards, I thought, "What an amazing thing to have done!" We even received a letter from one of the armed groups telling us that they shared our dream of a country where everyone would be treated with equality and live in freedom. They invited us to visit and talk about our work, but we never replied or took up the offer.

Six weeks later I went to Bogotá to take part in the first Children's Assembly. I met Farlis, Juan Elias, Mayerly, and many other young people who were doing wonderful work for peace in their communities. It was a time of great hope—especially when the Citizen's Mandate also got such strong support—but after the Mandates, things in Medellín seemed

....

cast my vote vote; make a choice
broke out began
justice fairness, lawfulness
eligible child voted child who could vote did vote

to **stall**. We had no **regular source of** information about what was happening in the Children's Movement in other parts of the country, so it was hard to keep that sense of unity.

I continued working in my church and community and gradually realized that the experience was changing me. I felt stronger and more confident. By the age of thirteen, I had begun advising women in my community who were victims of **domestic violence**. The adult workshops of the Corporación Regional had given me information about the laws and organizations that protected and supported abused women. I passed this information on to one or two women in the *barrio*, and they spread the word. Soon others were seeking me out, at the church, on the street, and at home. They trusted me at least partly because of my position as altar boy.

Many people in our neighborhood praised me and were grateful for the work I was doing, but at home I got nothing but criticism. Some of my relatives called me names and told me I was ignorant and weird because I spent time with young children. I tried not to let it affect me, but it hurt that my own family didn't understand or value what I was doing.

In October 1998, I went back to Bogotá for the second Children's Assembly, and I saw that the Movement was really **expanding**. I felt ashamed that we didn't have a better program organized in Medellín. John Fernando Mesa was also at that Assembly. He was a curator at a university in Medellín, and also worked with Redepaz. He also felt that Medellín should have a much stronger Children's Movement for Peace.

....

stall stop
regular source of way of getting
domestic violence violence at home
expanding growing

When we got back to the city, John Fernando, myself, and some other young people started working together. Through schools and youth organizations, we brought hundreds and then thousands more young people into the Movement. John Fernando **established a base** for the Children's Movement at the University of Antioquia in Medellín, where large numbers of kids from across the city would meet and talk about their experience and activities for peace. By 2000, more young people in Medellín were involved in some kind of community-based peace activity than probably anywhere else in the country. There still wasn't a lot of communication between all the groups, but we were making progress.

The Children's Movement for Peace was going well, but at home, things with Germán were still difficult. Fights **flared up out of nowhere**. He destroyed our clothes, threatened us with knives, and sometimes beat me or my sister. He always won the fights.

One night when I was fifteen, I was studying when Germán wanted to sleep. He told me to turn out the light. I refused, so he turned it out himself. I turned it on again. He removed the lightbulb, so I found another lightbulb and fitted it. He stood over me as I was working, pushing me, and saying, "So, you really want me to stick the knife in, do you? You want me to stab you?"

Something snapped inside me. I stood up, grabbed hold of him, and threw him against the wall. I rarely lose my temper,

----

established a base set up an office

flared up out of nowhere started for no reason

Something snapped inside me. I became very angry.

but I lost control completely and hit him again and again. He pushed me aside and tried to grab a knife, and I got even madder. I seized a bottle and hit him. I hit him with anything and everything I could lay my hands on. I hit him for every time he had terrorized me and made my life a misery. I hit him for attacking me and my sister when we were too young and weak to protect ourselves. I hit him with **every shred of power I possessed** until my brother and sister pulled me away.

Most of the fight happened in the dark. When the light came on, no one could believe what I'd done to him. Germán was supposed to be the "tough guy." I was supposed to be the "weakling." That night it all changed. I know that since I am a peacemaker, it should never have happened that way, but I was angry with him. I have never regretted what I did.

When my mother came home that night I told her everything, from beginning to end, all the things Germán had done to torment my sister and me, **unspeakable** things, and, of course, she was horrified. Of course she had never realized how bad it was. Of course she loved us and wanted to protect us, and right away she threw Germán out of our house. She tossed all his clothes into the street.

I should have talked to my mother sooner, but when I was young I didn't know **how to find the words**, I didn't have the confidence, and I didn't trust her.

She doesn't understand how I grew up the way I did. She told me, "You used to be such a brat but look at you now! You

....

every shred of power I possessed all of the strength that
I had

unspeakable awful, terrible

how to find the words what to say

are still a kid, but you think like an adult."

Recently, I noticed that she was becoming an alcoholic again. I don't mind if she has a drink now and then, but she was drinking every day, and too much of it. I waited until she was calm and sober, then asked her gently, "Mama, why are you drinking so much?"

"*¡Ave María!*" she sighed. "I'm bored. No one visits me. No one calls to say hello. Where are my children and grandchildren? I want to talk to them and have fun." They lived close by but hadn't spoken to her for **ages**.

I told her she was crazy. "You kill yourself working for us all, but you never complain. You just accept it. You should let them know how you feel."

"You don't understand," she told me. "You haven't had the experience I have had."

I could imagine her looking back over the tragic landscape of her life, beginning with the loss of Fredy. She'd lost that child three times over, once when Gloria's family took him, again when drugs took him, and again when he became a **fugitive**. The fathers of her children had abandoned her, and now her children were doing the same.

I said, "Well, I haven't had the same experience as you, but I've learned some things. I know that instead of spending your money on alcohol, you could buy a packet of *panela* [unrefined sugar cane] and some milk and bread. It would feed us a lot better than your drinking." But she just sighed. **I wasn't getting through.**

....

ages a long time

fugitive runaway; person who runs from the law

I wasn't getting through. She did not understand what I was saying to her.

"Okay," I told her, "I'll join *you* then. I'm failing my ethics class at school. Instead of giving me any dinner, why don't you just go out and get me a nice bottle of *aguadiente* [a very potent alcohol] so I can drink it, and then I'll be sure to pass my test tomorrow."

She laughed. "*¡Ave María!* it is better not to talk to you. You could **shut up the Devil himself**."

I help her with her money now. I also tried to speak to my siblings, asked them to visit her, but it broke down into an argument. They still haven't come. I hope one day they will understand.

I am sixteen years old and have been in the peace movement since I was twelve. I run child rights groups in several elementary schools, training kids to teach other children about their rights. I believe that if children grow up knowing and respecting their rights; if parents, teachers, and all adults respect and protect the rights of children; then we will transform our communities. We could even end the war.

I also work with a group of adolescents in the nearby *barrio* of La Planta. Adults around here are frightened by any group of young people, which they assume must be a gang of thieves or murderers. We try to challenge that **stereotype**, for instance, by organizing recreational activities for kids in the *barrio*. But it isn't easy because we have no **funds** and are working entirely on our own.

I've traveled to other countries to represent the Children's Movement for Peace, but I like Colombia better than any other

....

shut up the Devil himself make anyone realize their mistakes
stereotype common idea
funds money

place. It is tough here but life **is rich as well**. Overcoming the **hard knocks**, that is what makes you fall in love with life.

---

is rich as well can be good sometimes, too
hard knocks obstacles in life

BEFORE YOU MOVE ON...

1. **Comparisons** Reread pages 64–67. What was Beto's behavior like before and after he joined the movement?

2. **Conclusions** Reread pages 68–69. How did Beto get his mother to start understanding what she was doing wrong?

JOURNEYS FAR FROM HOME

It took weeks to figure out what had happened to Juanita. She couldn't tell it all at once. The story came out in pieces. **Her mind kept wandering.** Sometimes she cried so much we had to stop.

I met her at a Return to Happiness workshop, held in La Chinita, a *barrio* of Apartadó in northwest Colombia, that I was running with a handful of volunteers. The volunteers were all thirteen or fourteen years old. The kids were mostly under ten, and had been forced out of their homes in the surrounding villages by the violence. It was **ironic** that their families looked for safety in La Chinita, where some of the biggest massacres of the war had occurred.

Juanita was about seven years old, dark and plump, with tight black curls. She was a recent arrival in La Chinita and showed many signs of distress. When all the other kids were running around, playing games, singing songs, and painting pictures, Juanita sat on her own, sometimes watching the action, but mostly just staring at the dirt floor. Her face showed no expression, no feeling. **She looked numb and disconnected.**

The Return to Happiness project was set up by UNICEF and the Catholic Church in 1997 after violence in our region

....

Her mind kept wandering. She could not concentrate.

ironic unusual, unexpected

She looked numb and disconnected. She did not seem to care about anything.

forced thousands of families to flee from their homes. The project trained hundreds of teenagers and adults **as volunteer "play" therapists, who ran** workshops for displaced children. Each workshop followed the same basic pattern. First there were games and songs, then painting, and then we played with toys. Usually we played in groups but with kids like Juanita, the really sad ones, we played **one-on-one**.

I sat on the floor beside her and showed her the *bolsillo*, the knapsack full of materials that every volunteer carries. "Look what I've got in here," I told her, but she didn't seem interested.

I took out the rag dolls, the puppets, and the wooden toys—the donkey cart, the helicopter, the truck, the motorbike, and the boat. I started to play with them. I sat the man on the donkey cart and pushed him along. I flew the helicopter. I put the rag mother with the rag children and let them hug one another. Then I offered her the rag family.

She looked at them for a while, then she picked up the rag man and sat him on the donkey cart. She pushed him along, then burst into tears.

"Don't worry," I told her. "We can play again later."

She didn't answer, but she sat quietly while I read aloud the story of "The Happy Monkey." This is about a monkey who wants to be brave and strong but the only way he knows how to do this is to be aggressive. None of the other animals like him, but eventually, with the help of a wise **macaw**, he learns how to be a true friend, by trusting others.

While I told the story I used the puppets of the monkey

....

as volunteer "play" therapists, who ran to play with children and help them feel better, and to lead

one-on-one with them alone

macaw parrot

and the wise macaw to **illustrate** their roles. I introduced the macaw puppet to Juanita as a special friend that she could tell secrets to. Some of the kids find it easier to talk to a puppet than they do to a real person.

That first time I don't think Juanita took in half of what I was saying, but the first lesson of doing this work is that you have to give the kids time. Afterwards, I always sat with Juanita when we held a workshop in La Chinita. At first she didn't talk at all. Then she began to mumble, speaking through the toys. She often broke down and couldn't go on. Finally, after weeks of playing, I thought I understood the painful story of what had happened to her family.

The family was on the donkey cart: her father, her mother, Juanita, and her sister. A helicopter came and flew around them, making a loud whirring sound. When she flew the wooden helicopter, Juanita made the whirring sound through her teeth. **Her whole face was screwed up with the effort.**

The family was frightened by the noise and the way the helicopter circled overhead. Her father stopped the cart and they all ran away to hide in the banana fields. She was with her mother and sister. Her father was on the other side of the road.

The helicopter landed some way off. The men came and one of them found her father. Juanita and her mother and sister stayed hidden, but they saw everything. She saw them drag her father out of the field. She bent the tiny rag arms of the rag doll behind his head, just the way her father's arms had been. The commander of the armed men came along and he pushed

....

illustrate show

Her whole face was screwed up with the effort. Her face showed a lot of pain and anger as she made the helicopter sound.

Juanita's father onto the ground, facedown. Then he took out a gun and shot him three times. Every time the rag man went "pow!" with his gun, his whole body jumped with the force of his weapon. The rest of the family watched helplessly from their hiding places.

After the armed men had gone, Juanita gathered the rag dolls that **stood for** herself, her sister, and her mother, and ran them to the father doll. They fell on him and cried and cried until their mother said they must go, must leave, must run away. They fled, abandoning everything, and traveled first by boat and then in the back of a truck, until they came to La Chinita.

There wasn't much I could do to help Juanita, aside from playing with her, paying attention to her, and encouraging her to join in with the other kids. I had been trained to keep notes on how she was playing, what she seemed to be saying, and how her mood was, and I gave this information to the **project psychologist**. But the psychologist was overwhelmed. So many children were affected by the war, and some were even more disturbed than Juanita. It was quite a long time before the psychologist **got around to** her. By that time, Juanita seemed to be improving, sometimes even joining in our games. Then one day she just disappeared with her family. Probably they went to another town or even to the city, but no one knew for sure. It happens a lot these days. People are here and then they leave and you never find out what happened to them.

There is a lot about this work that is very sad. Sometimes

....

stood for represented

project psychologist doctor who studied the children's behavior

got around to had time to help

it is hard to **measure any kind of improvement in** the kids. It is hard to know if we are really achieving anything. I've sometimes thought about giving it all up because I need to spend more time on my studies. My family is also poor, and so I need to earn money to buy supplies for school. But I also wonder what would happen to these children if I and other young people didn't do this work. Most psychologists and **sociologists** don't want to come to Apartadó to work because they say it is too dangerous.

I was born in Montería, a large town about ninety miles east of Apartadó. My father had a small shop where he sold household goods and fixed motorbikes. We never had much money. My father often came home drunk, got into fights with my mother, cursed, and sometimes whipped me. When I was nine he left us and I never saw him much after that. A few years later he was murdered during a robbery. I was angry with him for abandoning us, but his death meant I lost him forever. I still miss him.

We had no money after my father left, so my mother began selling our household goods and furniture to buy food. Then she started selling her clothes. One day she told me she had to leave for a while, so that we could **make a new start** somewhere else. She wanted me to stay in the house in Montería. My mother promised to send me money and to telephone every week, then she left. I was ten years old, and for nearly a year I lived entirely alone.

....

measure any kind of improvement in know if you are helping
sociologists people who study human behavior
make a new start have a better life

I missed my mother desperately. I cried hard whenever I saw a photograph of her, or some of her clothes. I had to learn how to cook for myself, standing on a chair because I couldn't reach the stove. I washed my own clothes by hand and cleaned the house. I decided that if I was very good, took care of the house, and studied hard at school, my mother might come back. She called every week but she always asked me to wait a bit longer. I knew she had good reasons for being away, but I was miserable. I never told anyone I was alone, not even my friends or my teachers. I was afraid that if anyone knew, then robbers would come and my mother would never return.

She left me in February, 1995, and came back the following December. I couldn't believe it when she walked through the door. I held onto her, touching and hugging her. She had been thin when she went away, but she came back quite plump. She told me that we were going to live on a banana plantation near Apartadó. She had a job selling meals to the workers, and she was living with a man who would become my stepfather.

The tiny house that my mother took me to was unlike any other place I had ever lived. Montería was noisy and crowded. There were always people out on the streets, music blasting from bars, people selling anything and everything on the sidewalks. But the plantation was quiet and slow by day. Nothing ever happened there, and I wasn't used to the sounds of the countryside by night.

I'd heard that armed groups sometimes came to farms like that and **abducted** children who were then forced to become

....

abducted stole, took

soldiers. I'd heard of massacres of farm workers and I suffered from recurring nightmares in which an armed group appeared on the farm, dragged us out of our house, and killed us all. It was also strange to be living so closely with my mother and this man. He wasn't bad to me, but I felt like **an intruder**. I realized that even though I had missed my mother, I had almost become used to being alone.

After only a few weeks, my mother explained to me that I would have to leave. It was for my own good, she said, because I needed to go to a decent school. She had arranged for me to live with a cousin in Apartadó and to enter the ninth grade at the José Celestino Mutis secondary school. I didn't complain. Apartadó wasn't as big as Montería but at least it was a town.

Looking back, I know that even though I suffered when I was left alone, it also forced me to grow up quickly. Now I was determined to do well, study hard, and **get ahead**.

Soon after entering the school, I was elected to represent my class in the student government. A couple of months later, in April, 1996, Graça Machel came to Apartadó. That visit transformed a lot of our lives, because it **put Apartadó on the map as** a place where young people were really trying to do something to make peace. Many of us trained as promoters of the rights of children. We went into schools and taught other kids about their rights and why we should all vote in the Children's Mandate.

Really big changes began happening for me in 1997 when I was thirteen years old and the Return to Happiness program

....

an intruder I did not belong

get ahead become successful

put Apartadó on the map as made other people notice that Apartadó was

started. By that time, many displaced families were turning up in Apartadó, Turbo, and other towns in the region. Every day we would see them arrive on donkey carts, in trucks and buses, or on foot. There were old people, babies, young children, pregnant women. Many were wounded, emotionally if not physically, and stunned from what had happened to them. All they had left were the things they were carrying. They had been **driven from** their homes by the struggle between the armed groups who were competing for control of the land. These groups used the most **vicious methods** to force people to leave. They didn't care what happened to the children or what they saw: They would even kill the parents in front of the children and then leave the children with the bodies.

Most of the displaced moved in with relatives, rented small rooms, or **constructed** their own shelters. In a few places, special camps were set up. The municipal sports center in Turbo, a town about twenty miles from Apartadó, was transformed into a **massive dormitory** for about four hundred people.

As Return to Happiness volunteers we were given training, supplies, and T-shirts identifying us as part of the program. The demand for the workshops was huge. I recruited a dozen other volunteers from the Celestino School, helped in their training, and then organized the workshops that we ran in La Chinita and elsewhere. During 1997–1998, our group worked with more than a thousand children, and we were always getting requests to do more.

Even if it was hard, working in the program gave us

....

driven from forced out of
vicious methods violent ways
constructed made
massive dormitory large living area

something constructive to do in a situation where we could otherwise feel quite helpless. Also, trying to understand the difficulties of these children helped me to understand my own problems. I had always found it hard to talk about what had happened to me when my mother left and when my father was murdered, but listening to other kids helped me to **open up**.

By the time I began volunteering in the Return to Happiness program, I was living in a *barrio* known as Primero de Mayo (First of May) because that was the day on which squatters had invaded and seized the land. My mother and stepfather had been among them and together we had built a small wooden house.

Although I lived in Primero de Mayo, I had chosen to run the workshops in La Chinita because that was where many displaced children were living. But Apartadó was a deeply divided town. Different *barrios* **were often associated with support for** particular armed groups. People were sometimes suspicious of those who came from other *barrios*. It didn't make sense to some that we would do this work just to help children—any children.

After about a year of working in La Chinita, I began to receive threats. People told me, "We hear it is getting risky for you over here." I got anonymous phone calls telling me that I wasn't welcome in La Chinita anymore, or that I should **"look out for my health."** When I left my house, I felt as if I were being followed, although I never had any proof. I didn't

....

open up share my feelings and thoughts

were often associated with support for belonged to and supported

"look out for my health" be careful that I do not get hurt

know if the risk was real or not. Maybe it was just "talk," but I became so frightened I couldn't sleep at night or concentrate on my studies. Everything seemed suspicious. I spoke with the coordinator of the Return to Happiness program, and it was decided that I should stop working in La Chinita. I concentrated instead on trying to improve conditions for children in my own *barrio*—I developed a proposal and raised the funds that allowed us to put up a playground. I also volunteered at the office of the Return to Happiness program and for a while, produced a newsletter about different activities of youth volunteers. Via fax and eventually the Internet, **we were able to keep at least some young people in the region in touch with** what was happening in the Children's Movement for Peace in other parts of the country.

The idea that teenagers should play an active role in peacemaking had been an important **principle** for us in Apartadó ever since the visit of Graça Machel, but adults interpret "participation" in different ways. Some adults were sympathetic and believed in us; they listened to our ideas and tried to work with us. Others thought that because we were "only children" we should do as we were told. They felt that our opinions counted for nothing.

When Gloria Cuartas was the mayor of Apartadó, she really wanted to work with young people. It was because of her that Farlis became the first Child Mayor of Apartadó in April 1996. At the same time, even though I was only twelve years old, I had become the Secretary General of the children's government

....

we were able to keep at least some young people in the region in touch with some of the young people in the area were able to know

principle belief

of Apartadó. We thought that this children's government was an important breakthrough for young people in the town. Gloria Cuartas **was always receptive to hearing about** our ideas and experiences. But when she left office and another mayor took over, we no longer had the same access. We had no rights under the law to have our opinions **taken into account**. It depended entirely on the personal views of the adults concerned.

We never had any more elections for the children's government in Apartadó (although these have been held successfully in other towns in Colombia). Farlis kept the title of Child Mayor until she turned eighteen, and then there was no more Child Mayor. I am now sixteen and still use my title of Secretary General sometimes, because it can help. I used it just a few weeks ago to help my school donate several blackboards to a very poor school in another *barrio*. Yet my title as Secretary General **is really an empty one**, because there is no other official left in the children's government except me.

I had been working in the peace movement for more than four years, and frankly I had become quite depressed. My life had become so serious. I felt unable to have fun like other young people. If I wasn't studying, I was selling hot dogs to make money to buy school supplies, or working with children, or volunteering at the Return to Happiness office. I never went dancing. I never just hung out with other people my age, not unless it was to plan a peacemaking event. The work seemed endless.

....

was always receptive to hearing about always wanted to hear about

taken into account heard

is really an empty one does not really matter

Then, in September 2000, I was invited to go to the United Nations in New York to talk about my work. There were four of us representing the Children's Movement for Peace: Mayerly came from Bogotá, Sebastian from Medellín, Leonardo from Mapiripan, and myself. We talked about our lives and our work in front of many **United Nations delegates**, and showed the film *Soldiers of Peace: A Children's Crusade* that **CNN** had made about our Movement in 1999.

Each of us had different experiences of violence and very different ways of making peace. Leonardo, who is thirteen years old, talked about a terrible massacre in his village that forced everyone to leave. He went to Mapiripan with his family. There he got involved in a project that established "territories of peace" in public parks and playgrounds. These were areas where children could go to solve conflicts without violence.

Sebastian had been shot in the head "by mistake" during a gang attack on his father's taxi. He now worked with Beto in Medellín helping primary school children to understand their rights. I talked about the murder of my father, and told the story of Juanita using the dolls and wooden toys from the Return to Happiness project.

Many people praised our work and told us that we were brave. I never really felt brave, but experiencing how other people saw us helped me to understand that what we are doing is important. People were kind and generous to us and for a few days we **lived like tourists**. We went to the top of the World Trade Center, took a boat tour to the Statue of

....

United Nations delegates people from different countries that work for peace

CNN a famous television news show

lived like tourists visited famous and important places in New York

Liberty, and visited a huge amusement park. It was so different from everything I know in Apartadó—so beautiful and extraordinary, like an illusion, a dream.

Back in Apartadó life is very much the same as it was before. I **hold onto those images of** New York. I don't ever want to forget them—yet I **also feel as if my mind has been cleared of doubt**. Many people in other countries are interested in and care about our work. It is wonderful to feel their affection and support. I told the other volunteers in Apartadó that we have friends all over the world, more than we could possibly imagine.

Last week, ten of us sat down and planned a children's march against kidnapping. More than three hundred children and teenagers took part. We stopped the traffic as we walked through Apartadó calling for the right to life to be respected, for children to be kept out of the war, for our right to live in peace and freedom.

It was a great day.

....

hold onto those images of think a lot about the things I saw in

also feel as if my mind has been cleared of doubt now believe Colombia can have peace

BEFORE YOU MOVE ON...

1. **Inference** Reread pages 71–74. Why did Johemir use toys to help Juanita talk about her family?

2. **Cause and Effect** Reread pages 82–83. How did Johemir's trip to New York affect his motivation?

LETTERS FROM THE JUNGLE

The theater was massive and in the darkness it seemed to grow even **more cavernous**. We were huddled in family groups, hugging each other. Some people were already crying. The **colonel** walked up on the stage and read out the names of the sixty-one police officers and cadets who had been kidnapped during the **storming of** Mitú. With every name, a photograph appeared on the screen and one family group in the vast hall sighed or cried out because it was their son or husband or father or brother or lover.

I sat in the darkness with my father and mother and heard the Colonel speak "Hernando's" name. My mother gasped, "There he is!" His face appeared on the screen, looking like me as always, with the same nose and the same mouth. But this time he was looking back at us from far away, from a place we couldn't reach.

Then the camera slowly panned by all the faces, and each **captive** said a few words. Someone shouted out, "My son! My son is alive! What do I do now? My son is out there in the jungle!"

When Hernando came on the screen, it was as if everyone else in the theater disappeared, and he was there only for us.

....

more cavernous wider, larger
colonel military officer
storming of attack on
captive prisoner, victim

"Hello Mom, Dad, everyone," he said. "I'm doing fine. You don't have to worry. I miss you all very much but I'll be released soon. You just get on with your lives and **don't let your spirits get you down** because I'm going to be just fine. . . ."

Hernando's kidnapping has changed everything. **It holds all of us hostage.** We cannot think about anything else. I don't have conversations with my mother anymore because I know, before I begin, what she is thinking. The kidnapping colors all my dreams. When I eat I think, "What is he eating?" When I sleep I think, "How is he sleeping?"

Nothing can be right in our world until he comes back.

Hernando left school in 1994 and decided to join the police. He signed on to drive a patrol car. He never imagined he would be in combat. After his initial training he was supposed to join the highway police in Cartagena in the north. Then the commander called the new recruits to a meeting and asked which of them did not want to go to Cartagena. Now Cartagena is a beautiful coastal town, and one of Colombia's most popular tourist locations, but it is a long way from Bogotá. Hernando raised his hand, thinking that he would be posted closer to the capital. Instead he was told that he must go right away to Mitú. He had never even heard of the place.

Mitú is small **garrison town**, deep in the Amazon region, only thirty miles from the border with Brazil. For hundreds of miles in all directions, there is nothing but rivers and

....

don't let your spirits get you down do not let this situation make you sad

It holds all of us hostage. It is all we can think of.

garrison town town where the military camps out

the jungle. And Mitú is well inside territory that has been **contested** by the armed groups for more than forty years.

We were all afraid when Hernando was sent there, but for the first couple of years it turned out to be a peaceful place. Hernando made many friends and found a girlfriend. She worked at the hospital and also came from Bogotá. We have photographs of his life there. In one he is wearing swimming shorts and standing on the bank of the River Vaupés. Another shows him relaxed and happy with his fellow officers inside the police station.

Several journalists had been writing that Mitú had been threatened—and, given its location, I suppose it was inevitable that eventually the war would reach there—but none of us thought about it at the time. Hernando never **gave the impression** that there was any trouble. Even though he was so far away we spoke on the phone two or three times a week. In 1997 he came home **on leave** and stayed for a couple of months. He was due to come again on November 1, 1998, but that was the day that the town was attacked.

My mother was woken up that Sunday at dawn by a telephone call from my godfather. "Listen to the radio," he told her. "A battle is going on in Mitú."

My father was away, but my mother woke me up and we spent the whole day in the house, listening to the radio and waiting for news. My older sister came over and made calls to the Red Cross and other places trying to get information. At one point, my mother announced she had had enough. She

----

contested fought over
gave the impression let us know
on leave for vacation

was going to get on a plane and fly out there to see what was happening.

"You can't go, mama," my sister told her. "They are still fighting. It's a war zone."

So my mother went back to waiting. The tears rolled down her face. You could see she would not have minded walking right into the battle to pick up her son and bring him home.

She was thinking, "You can have your war, but let me have my child."

Instead we waited and learned that during the attack on the police station, all the officers **on duty** had been killed. We didn't know if Hernando had been on duty or not; we didn't know if he was alive or dead. The town was **virtually** destroyed. People fled in **droves**. Still, the news only came through in bits and pieces. Two weeks passed before we knew Hernando had been kidnapped, that in the midst of the fighting he had been loaded into the back of a truck, apparently asleep or unconscious, and covered with ash from the explosions.

Until we knew for sure that he was safe, I was **out of my mind with grief**. I wept constantly. At times I was sure he was dead, then just as convinced that he must be alive. I was sure he would have been terrified in combat. He didn't belong in the war. I think he hardly understood it. I don't think any of us understand it.

I stayed away from school for a few weeks, but when I went back I didn't tell anyone what had happened, not my teachers or my friends. I thought they wouldn't understand or care. My

....

on duty who were working
virtually almost completely
droves large numbers
out of my mind with grief feeling very confused and sad

teachers only found out weeks later when my mother went to a **PTA meeting** and told them. Afterwards they were more supportive and sometimes asked if there was news, but I felt as if a gulf had opened up between me and other people who had not been touched directly by the war. I thought they could not possibly imagine what it was like to **walk in my shoes**.

I was involved in the peace movement long before Hernando was kidnapped. In 1995, when I was ten years old, I joined the Colombian Red Cross as a volunteer and started learning about international human rights—the rights people have to protection during war, the rights of children, and so on. I also became involved in the Free Air program. I learned about the environment, about damage to the ozone layer, recycling, and the problems of deforestation. I became a "multiplier," which means I organized seminars at my own and at other schools to pass on this information. Through the Colombian Red Cross I received training in how to work with other young people in an entertaining way, using colorful brochures and games that were fun as well as educational.

I became much more involved in peace activities in 1997, when I was about twelve years old. This was the year that the Citizen's Mandate was held and **peace was suddenly on everyone's lips**. At the Red Cross, a group of young volunteers were interviewed about our ideas towards peace. Their questions inspired me.

I decided that peace was really a state of mind. Peace

....

PTA meeting meeting for parents and teachers

walk in my shoes live my life

peace was suddenly on everyone's lips suddenly everyone was talking about peace

depended on the way you saw things and on how you responded to other people. If this was so, then it seemed to me that it should be possible for children and young people to do quite a lot to make peace, even without the help of adults.

In the Children's Mandate of 1996, nearly three million children and adolescents had voted for their rights and for peace. The Mandate was important, but it was only the first step. If we really wanted to make peace, I thought, we would need to change the way we felt inside.

I was very excited by this idea. I thought, "I can have big goals even though I am a kid."

I set up my peace project without the help of any other organization or adults, although the Red Cross was always helpful. To get permission to run peace seminars at my school, I had to write letters to the **rector** and create a plan of action showing what I wanted to do, when I wanted to do it, and what the activities would be. Some teachers were doubtful whether other students would be interested, but plenty were. Mostly they were interested in **themes like peaceful coexistence within the** school and how we could get more unity. But I also used these sessions to promote the idea that peace is not just a word, it is something that we can all do.

I tried to keep the meetings dynamic. I knew from my other work with the Red Cross that I would get nowhere if I gave boring lectures. Gradually I began **branching out into** other schools and even organized some big meetings where large numbers of students got together to share ideas.

....

rector priest

themes like peaceful coexistence within the ideas like how people with different ideas can get along in

branching out into going to

Sometimes I was able to help individual students. One girl called "Ana Dolores" had a lot of problems at home, where she was very badly abused. As a result, she was aggressive and destructive at school and was badly treated there as well. Her classmates often humiliated her.

I invited Ana Dolores to come to a forum that I was running during recess in the school theater. After that she began to trust and **confide in me**. That was how I learned about the abuse. She had never told anyone before.

Soon afterwards I arranged to give a talk to her class. I didn't identify Ana Dolores by name, but **in a roundabout way I inferred** that I was talking about her. I described some of the problems of living in a violent home and how this could make a person behave in a certain way at school. I said we could all help that person by understanding and listening to them. After that things changed. Her classmates became much more supportive, and Ana Dolores became happier, at least at school.

After Hernando's kidnapping, the peace project became much more important to me. I think the other students also took me more seriously because they knew I was affected by violence. It made them more interested. But I lost most of my friends because I stopped joking around in class. I also stopped going out unless it was to a peace meeting, or to volunteer for the Red Cross. I've mostly worked alone on the peace project, but recently more students have been asking what they can do to get involved.

....

confide in me share her thoughts and feelings with me

in a roundabout way I inferred gave hints without telling exact details

I dream only good dreams about Hernando—that I walk into the house and he is by my side.

I lie on my bed, stare at the ceiling, and try to imagine where he is now, what he is doing.

I think about our lives growing up. **I am sometimes even nostalgic for** the fights we had, over who would get into the bathroom first or over the way he used to pull the blankets off me when I was sleeping.

Sometimes I see someone who looks like him in the street and **my heart jumps**.

I wonder what it will be like for him when he comes back, how will he cope after being in the jungle for two years or more, without even seeing a bus?

I feel good about the peace work because I'll be able to show Hernando that I didn't sit around with my arms crossed while he was **in captivity**.

Three months after the kidnapping, we heard that police headquarters had received a videotape and letters from the victims of the Mitú kidnapping. At the time we thought that perhaps Hernando would be released soon. Many times since then negotiations have been held with the armed group holding him, yet years have passed and he is still not free. My mother got involved with *Asofamilas*, a support organization for families of the Mitú kidnap victims, and has participated in some negotiations herself. At least we have been able to send books, photos, and letters to him, and receive letters back.

....

I am sometimes even nostalgic for Sometimes I miss
my heart jumps I get excited
in captivity in prison

So many people have been kidnapped in Colombia that a special radio station has been set up so that people can send messages to their loved ones in captivity. We have been on *Radio Recuerdo* (Radio Remember) and sent messages to Hernando. We know he has heard us.

In one letter he wrote, "It's wonderful to hear your voices [on the radio] and know that everybody is fine. Every night I wait for the program to start and listen to see if someone says hi to me. . . ."

He told us about his life. "Every day they wake us up at 6 A.M. to have breakfast and then you're left **'deprogrammed'** because there's nothing to do apart from lie in a **hammock** thinking. . . . I play dominos but I get tired of playing them all the time even though there are some friends here who play like crazy all day long."

I have sent poems to him, to inspire him to stay confident and hopeful. I tell him that I listen to his advice and study hard. I was very glad when he recently wrote back and said, "I am happy you're doing so well at school. . . . That's where I went wrong. I regret not having made the most of my studies. . . . I really didn't like reading, for example . . . [yet] here I have read over thirty books of all different kinds and there are still more to read. I even get the dictionary and look up weird words that I don't know. . . . I would never have done this **of my own accord** before. . . ."

Even though he seems safe, I still worry. You never know what will happen. If I could talk to the people who are holding

....

'deprogrammed' bored

hammock cloth hanging bed

of my own accord on my own

my brother I would ask them to have **compassion** and to understand the suffering they have caused.

I think that forgiveness is **fundamental** if we are to achieve peace. The war cannot come to an end without forgiveness. It is especially important for people like us who have suffered to forgive.

I think that this is what I am working for—I work for forgiveness.

....

compassion sympathy
fundamental important, crucial

BEFORE YOU MOVE ON...

1. **Summarize** How did Alberto inspire others to work harder in the peace movement?

2. **Evidence and Conclusions** Alberto was a person who was motivated and creative. List 3 examples to support this.

where are we now?

The first edition of this book was published in 2001. In this section, the author writes about the things that had changed in the Children's Movement for Peace in Colombia and in the lives of the peace activists whose stories appear in this book up to the year 2001.

The Children's Movement for Peace now has more than 100,000 **active** members. Many come into the Movement through the church, the Colombian Scouts, the Colombian Red Cross, Redepaz, YMCA, World Vision, and other organizations. But anyone under the age of eighteen, doing anything to help **improve the quality of life** in a community affected by violence, is considered an automatic member of the Movement. In Spring 2000, newspaper advertisements invited children and teenagers across the country to sign on with the Movement and describe their activities for peace. It drew tens of thousands of replies.

Most members interviewed for *Out of War* said that the biggest problem facing the Movement is lack of communication. Most are **without easy access to** telephones and computers, so they have to depend on adults to keep them informed about activities of the Movement in other parts of the country.

....

active working
improve the quality of life make life better for people
without easy access to not able to use

After his father was murdered, Juan Elias and his family continued to receive threats. In 1997, these became so intense that they decided to leave Aguachica and try to begin a new life in a new town. But the threats continued. They have been forced to move several times since, always suddenly and in secret. Juan Elias would like to study law and human rights at a university, but the current circumstances of his family have made this difficult. He insists that no matter what happens, he will continue working for peace.

In August 2000, Luis Fernando Rincón, the former mayor of Aguachica, who helped to inspire Juan Elias to work for peace, was assassinated.

Farlis, the outspoken daughter of a banana plantation worker, became a powerful spokesperson for the Children's Movement for Peace. Until she turned eighteen in 1999, she was its most visible representative. Farlis traveled to many countries, addressing audiences that sometimes numbered in the thousands, and occasionally included presidents and Nobel **laureates**.

Everywhere she has told the stories of the Children's and Citizen's Mandates, explaining that "at certain times, when countries fall into very great difficulties, children can hold the key to the future." She has talked about the meaning of peace for children, and how having peace at home and in the community is just as important as making peace in the war.

Farlis graduated from high school and for a while was uncertain if she would be able to fulfill her dream of going to

....

laureates prize winners

college. In 1999, Colombia's prestigious University of the Andes awarded her a scholarship. She is now studying psychology in Bogotá and hopes to **work in the rehabilitation** of former child soldiers and other children traumatized by war.

For the other young people whose stories are told in this book, life remains much the same. "Alberto" continues to wait for the return of his brother. "We have just passed the second anniversary of the kidnapping."

Johemir and other volunteers in the Return to Happiness program received special recognition from the Women's Commission for Refugee Women and Children in 1999. The Commission honored the Movement with its "Voices of Courage" award for its services to displaced families.

Beto and Johemir would love to be able to go to college, but their opportunities are limited by lack of funds. Beto would also like to work with children in a poorer country. Johemir feels trapped by poverty. He is afraid that when he graduates from high school next year he will be forced to enter the army. "No one in my country can refuse to fight **as a matter of conscience**."

....

work in the rehabilitation help change the lives

as a matter of conscience because they do not believe in war

BEFORE YOU MOVE ON...

1. **Summarize** Reread pages 94–96. How are the peace activists in the Movement doing? How are they struggling?

2. **Author's Point of View** Why did the author include this chapter?

acknowledgments

The Children's Movement For Peace is an orginization of young people, but it would have had far less impact without the vision of Cecilio Adorna and Nidya Quiroz of UNICEF and Ana Teresa Bernal from the Redepaz peace network. They took risks and dedicated the resources that allowed the Movement to grow.

Most of us would know little of the Children's Movement for Peace if José Ramos Horta had not had the imagination and courage to nominate it for a Nobel Peace Prize. José has nominated the Movement four times since 1998 and says he will continue to do so "until they win."

The Children's Movement for Peace would not exist without the hard work of thousands of young people. Many thanks to all those who shared their lives and dreams so that this book could be written. Many more stories remain to be told. Special thanks to Dilia from Redepaz; to Gloria, Iván Darío, and Gabriel of the Scouts in Bogotá; to Erika Vanessa, Victoria, Paula Marcela, and other Scouts of Caquetá; to Camila and other Scouts of Cali; to Marta, Monica, Diego, and other children from World Vision; to Erika, Lelis Isabel, and others at Benposta; to Javier, Camilo Andrés, and other students at the Colegio de San Bartolomé; to Cristian Camilo at the Fundación

Rafael Pombo; to Juan Carlos, Lina María, and others at the Colombian Red Cross; to Alexander, Tani, Diana, and others in Urabá; to Linia and other *semilleros* in Medellín; to Judy, Jhon Fredy, and others in the peace program of San Cristóbal; to Juan Carlos, Andrea, and others of the YMCA in Bogotá; to Jairo, Carmen, and others at the Talleres de Vida; to Leidy Diana of the Organización Pro Niña Indefensa; to Jhon, the stilt walker, Paolo, and others in Armenia; to Nicolas, Natalia, and others from the Escuelas de Paz; to Angela, Sandra, Julio, Miguel Angel, and others of the Phoenix program in Medellín; to Paola, Beatriz Elena, María del Carmen, and others at the Mama Margarita Institute in Medellín; to César, Juan David, Tomás, Juan Daniel, and others in Cali; to Alex, María Alejandra, and others in Carambolas; to Daicy, Daniela, and others at the Arzobispo Garcia School in Medellín, and to Alexander, Fabián, and others from Corabastos Market. Thanks also to all the other children who participated in the workshops in Bogotá, Medellín, Cali, Apartadó, Turbo, Florencia-Caquetá, Florida Blanca, and Bucaramanga.

I cannot express enough thanks to Cecilio Adorna and Nidya Quiroz for bringing me to Colombia. I am profoundly grateful to Patricia Lone, Chief of Publications at UNICEF Headquarters, who gave the book creative space, time, and endless encouragement. Carel de Rooy and Clara Marcela Barona from UNICEF Colombia gave me accommodation, advice, support and, most precious of all, their friendship. Many other UNICEF staff gave valuable support, especially Marjorie Newman Williams, Bill Hetzer, Ruth Landy, Ellen Tolmie,

Jeanette Gonzalez, Encke King, Loch Phillips, Margaret Kyenkya Isabirye, César Romero, and Susana Sánchez.

I was continually amazed by the warmth and willingness of Colombians to explain their much-misunderstood country. I am grateful to Ana Teresa Bernal, Diego Luis Arias, and others of Redepaz; "Pacho" Santos of El Tiempo; Antanas Mockus, now Mayor of Bogotá; Augusto Ramírez Ocampo, now Minister for Development; Héctor Fabio Henao and Alberto Maldonaldo of the Conferencia Episcopal; Leomidas Moremo, Pilar Plaza Queralt, Hildemaro Cruz, and others in Urabá; Carlos Castellanos of CINEP; Leonidas Manuel López of the Corporación Regiónal in Medellín; John Fernando Mesa of the University of Antioquia; Edith Cecilia Vega and others of the Colombian Red Cross; María Eugenia Ramírez and others of the Defense for Children International; Jorge Rojas of CODHES; Estella Duque Cuesta and Denis de Rojas of Talleres de Vida; José Luis Campos of Benposta; Clara Teresa Cárdenas de Arbelaez of Fundación Rafael Pombo; Oswaldo Ardila, Edgar Flores, and Rosalba Perez of World Vision; Pedro Patiño of Profamilia; Nydia Arguello, Myriam Orozco, and others at the YMCA; Luz Amanda Ortiz of Corporacíon Convivencia; Emilia Casas and others in the Colombian Scout Movement, including Javier Nieto in Cali and Oscar Gutierrez Agudelo and others in Caquetá.

Thanks also to Ambassador Alfonso Valdivieso and Ambassador Andrés Franco of the Permanent Mission of Colombia to the United Nations; Hernando Ramos and others of the Phoenix Program in Medellín, Sister Martha Isabel

Minotta of the Hermanitas de la Asunción; Fabiola Ochoa of the Mama Margarita Institute; Martha Isabel Quintero from the Casa de Juventud, Armenia; Amada Benavides of the Escuelas de Paz; Fernando Cardona at the Colegio Bello Oriente, Carambolas; Franklin Daza and David Macías Scarpeta of the Colegio Iván Darío López, Cali; María Auxilio Gallo of the Arzobispo García School in Medellín; Juan Barbero, Jorge Camacho, Otty Patiño, León Valencia, and Francisco Ortíz.

Kathy Eldon, Amy Eldon, Kyra Thompson, Lydia Smith, and others made *Soldiers of Peace* into a powerful and inspirational documentary.

I am grateful and indebted to the enthusiasm, dedication, commitment, and empathy of Marina Curtis-Evans, as well as her skill with both languages.

Most of all, love and thanks to my husband, George McBean, and our children, Fergus, Ainslie, and Ramsay—who always "understand."

I have done my best to tell these stories truthfully. Any faults are my own.